Wild Men, Wild Alaska

Wild Men, Wild Alaska

Finding What Lies Beyond the Limits

Rocky McElveen

NELSON BOOKS
A Division of Thomas Nelson Publishers
Since 1798
www.thomasnelson.com

Published in Nashville, Tennessee, by Thomas Nelson, Inc.

Nelson Books Titles may be purchased in bulk for educational, business, fund-raising, or sales promotional use. For information, please email SpecialMarkets@ThomasNelson.com.

Library of Congress Cataloging-in-Publication Data

McElveen, Rocky.
    Wild men, wild Alaska : finding what lies beyond the limits / Rocky
McElveen.
        p. cm.
    ISBN 0-7852-1772-X (hardcover)
    1. Men—Religious life. 2. Fishing—Religious aspects—Christianity.
3. Hunting—Religious aspects—Christianity. 4. Fishing—Alaska. 5. Hunting—
Alaska. I. Title.
BV4528.2.M34 2006
248.8'42—dc22   2005036822

Printed in the United States of America

05 06 07 08 09 QW 5 4 3 2 1

To the Beauty in my life. . . . I never want to lose—Sharon.
And to our four incredible daughters . . . Ginger Glory,
Merilee Joy, Kelly Grace and Sunny Faith, our "Virtue
Sisters," you all are the greatest adventure in my life.

CONTENTS

A Foreword by Franklin Graham

Awhile back my friend Rocky McElveen read to me from a stack of papers. They were chicken scratch stories of his adventures over the past decades as one of Alaska's infamous hunting and fishing guides. Little did I know that I would be hearing an early version of Rocky's book, the one you're currently holding.

When you crack the pages of *Wild Men, Wild Alaska*, you'll be captivated by the true-to-life depictions of majestic mountains, pristine lakes and streams, wild animals, hair-raising brushes with death . . . and how that all relates to a person's need for an adventurous connection with God.

Rocky writes in a down-to-earth style. He's honest, friendly, and as electrified as a kid just before the roller coaster drops. When he fails, you'll know it. When he's scared, you'll feel it. When he and his clients succeed, you'll sense the triumph and be stirred to triumph yourself.

You will be challenged by stories that reveal a God who is an everpresent help in times of trouble. You will be moved by Alaska's splendor that compels us to seek meaning and purpose. At its deepest level, *Wild Men, Wild Alaska* shares the teachings of Christ through a guide's experiences. These are modern day parables with a dose of adrenaline.

For those dazed by materialism and comfort, listlessly circling in the "rat race," this book is more than an escape. It's a defibrillator on a fatigued life. It invites you to escape a couch potato existence and challenges you to travel down your own trails on a more passionate path.

Parents, I think this book should permanently be on your child's nightstand. Rocky's stories charm, excite, teach by example, and cause reflection. They are a great way to ignite imaginations and adventurous spirits. Plus, this warm and touching series of narratives shows the true events God uses to bring a family closer and stretch them further spiritually.

I have hunted and fished with Rocky many times over the years. I know him as a friend, fellow traveler, and man with a great heart for adventure. God wants you to experience life to its fullest, and *Wild Men, Wild Alaska* is an account of one man who has fearlessly gripped a full life. I am pleased that he now passes his stories on to stir us to the same pursuit. Rocky has taken the "wild" from the Alaskan wilderness and put it into your hands.

As an outdoorsman and pilot who understands risks, it's my pleasure to introduce you to a friend who has dared to find what lies beyond the limits. As Rocky says to his clients, "Let your *guide* be your *conscience!*" Let this Alaskan guide lead you into the heart of a revitalizing experience, the journey of *Wild Men, Wild Alaska*.

Alaska is a beautiful but cruel mistress.

The beauty of the land, the majesty of the mountains, the sheer wild vastness of this last frontier are a constant lure to the adventurer.

But sometimes the results of these adventures are known only by God.

Introduction

I stood in the back of the boat, paralyzed by fear. My terrified partner was huddled in the bow, which was inexplicably lodged against the riverbank. Mere feet away, towering above us, was a huge, roaring, nine-foot grizzly bear. He stood on his hind legs, massive arms swinging back and forth, foaming at the mouth, nostrils flaring, eyes blazing, and ebony-sharp teeth gleaming in the early morning light. Water from his recent swim dripped from long, sharp claws. I hoped my blood would not soon be dripping from them.

It had taken only moments for us to drift from the comparative safety of the river into a death trap. Silently I prayed for mercy, knowing that the next few seconds would determine whether we would suffer a painful, cruel death by mauling or somehow be spared. The choice was not mine to make. It was up to this beautiful, powerful, angry beast—and God.

Since 1957 I have been a part of the great state of Alaska, making the journey from young man to longtime professional guide and outfitter.

I have experienced the beauty and known all too well the bitter cruelty of the Alaskan wilderness. These stories are my recollections of incredible encounter and survival. These adventures have changed the lives of everyone caught up in them. They have greatly impacted relationships with my family and friends and have deeply strengthened my faith journey, compelling me to search deeper and deeper.

In his best-selling book *Wild at Heart*, John Eldredge talks about the inevitable inward search that is caused by the wild outdoors and hunting. He says, "That is why I come. That is why I linger here still, letting the old bull get away. My hunt, you see, has little to do with elk. I knew that before I came. There is something else I am after, out here in the wild. I am searching for an even more elusive prey . . . something that can only be found through the help of wilderness. I am searching for my heart."[1]

In his book, Eldredge suggests that one of the things all men long for is an adventure to live. A man needs adventure to discover the secret of his soul. Well, these stories will prove that Eldredge's concepts are indeed dead-on. I have seen men discover their souls through real-life adventures, and I believe there is a deep longing in every man to test his limits and discover who he really is.

But this book is not just about men, for men. Women, this book is for you too. Unlike other hunting and fishing books, the following pages will give you amazing insights into every man and why adventure is—and, yes, why *love* is—important to him. To all who read this, come join me on my continuing journey, where men must pit their strength, their wits, their lives, and ultimately, their faith, against the unpredictable wildness of Alaska, and in so doing, find their true hearts.

ONE

The Call of the Wild

My mother was known by her friends as a "fishing and hunting widow." That's because my missionary/pastor father loved to hunt and fish in the Deep South, where we lived. Mom had rarely been out of the Deep South—rarely out of Mississippi, for that matter. So when Dad announced that he had experienced "God's call" to Alaska—and that he was taking her, his three sons, and his toddler daughter to live there—she just stared at him, wide-eyed.

As we were leaving for Alaska in our 1957 Chevy Nomad station wagon, Mom wondered whether it was the "call of the Lord" or just the "call of the wild," because no matter where we lived, whenever Dad prayed about God providing for the family, it meant we needed to grab our hunting rifles and fishing poles. I'll never forget Dad's favorite missionary prayer after we arrived in Alaska: "Dear Lord, You are great and powerful. This is a tough land, but in it You have created salmon, moose, and caribou. We ask that You make a place for them . . . right next to my mashed potatoes!"

From Mississippi to Alaska's Kenai Peninsula is close to five thousand miles by road. And the year 1957 was long before hordes of tourists made the summer trek to Alaska. We traveled over rough roads—gravel roads, dirt roads, icy roads, and then the Alaskan-Canadian Highway.

During World War II, Japan invaded Alaska and was occupying some of the Aleutian Islands. The Alaska Highway project was launched to move defense supplies from the U.S. mainland to Alaska. The construction of the sixteen-hundred-mile-long Alaska Highway began at Dawson Creek, British Columbia, and would terminate in Anchorage. From Seattle to Dawson Creek, British Columbia is roughly seven hundred miles of primitive road, making the trip from Seattle to Anchorage over twenty-three hundred miles of unmapped wilderness travel. The construction of the "Alcan" was heralded as a near-impossible engineering feat. Many likened it to the building of the Panama Canal. That's because the engineers had so many challenges. One was the soft, marshy tundra. Solid ground had to be found before the road's surface could be laid. Another challenge was the permafrost (permanently frozen ground a few feet below the tundra). It wreaked havoc when dug through, because it would turn into mud and acres of water. To combat this, tons of sand were required to insulate the roadbed.

There was much praise for the soldiers who completed the Alcan in just eight months and twelve days. Ill-housed, often living in tents, with insufficient clothing and bland food, they worked twenty-hour days through a punishing winter. Temperatures hovered at -40°F for weeks at a time, with a record low of -79°F. The road, originally called the Alaskan-Canadian Highway, quickly adopted the shortened name: Alcan Highway. Today this road, known as the Alcan, still provides the only land route to Alaska.

Those who traveled the Alcan in the early years remember the road as a seemingly endless series of switchbacks continuing for miles at a time. That's because, mainly, the road was constructed using "sight engineering" (taking whatever route looked good to the eye) because of a lack of surveys, equipment, and experience. The result is that the Alcan is one of the most crooked roads ever built! (A potential benefit was, if a long army supply convoy ever came under air attack, the trucks presumably couldn't be taken out with one direct line of fire, as would be the case if the road were straight.)

Commemorating the frustration every Alcan traveler has felt, army sergeant Troy Hise wrote:

The Alaska Highway

Winding in and winding out
Fills my mind with serious doubt
As to whether "the lout"
Who planned this route
Was going to hell, or coming out!

After World War II, funds to maintain the Alcan were not available. It was no longer considered a defensive necessity for the United States or for Canada. By 1957 the road had seen twelve years of neglect. Rain, snow, ice, spring thaws, and frost heaves left the road a continuous string of potholes and washouts. It was a major trial even for the brave of heart. And in the 1950s, the only four-wheel-drive vehicles were either army supplied or homebuilt, neither of which applied to our station wagon. As the miles twisted by, we couldn't help but notice the crosses placed at near-regular intervals, much like those on the old wagon train trail from Kansas to Oregon. And like the scouts along that trail, we tried to find the best path through mud or washed-out roadways. On that forlorn stretch of road, travelers had to rely on one another. Other travelers would need assistance in pushing or towing their vehicles when stuck or broken down, and we received the same from them.

There is an old story about a poor preacher who breaks down on the highway and is bargaining with the mechanic about the cost of repairs. He says, "I can't afford these repairs. I am just a poor preacher." The mechanic replies, "Yeah, I know. I heard you last Sunday." Well, Dad was a fine preacher, but we were dirt-poor. We couldn't afford anything. While other travelers were looking for a motel as the sun was setting, Dad was spying out a camping spot by a river or stream where we could pitch our tent and he could fish for our supper. We had a slab of salt pork wrapped in canvas, a Coleman stove, blankets, and an old army-issue canvas tent that leaked anywhere it was touched—but we never missed a meal on that long trip.

Alaska Just Ahead

It would take several lifetimes to experience all Alaska has to offer. It is so vast that it makes the middle of nowhere look crowded. Alaskan sourdoughs (people who have lived in Alaska more than a year) like to remind Texans that if they divided Alaska in half, Texas would move down to the third-largest state.

Wildlife is abundant and incredible. There are huge Alaskan coastal brown bears, mean seven-foot black bears, man-eating grizzlies, mammoth polar bears, wicked wolves, fearless wolverines—and backstabbing ex-spouses. There are hundreds of species of birds, exotic plants, and tenacious tundra. The terrain is so rugged in places that it has never been fully surveyed except by air. Alaska also boasts extremes in weather, and the temperature range can be nearly 180 degrees. There is more rainfall and snow in Alaska than in almost any inhabited area in the world. Alaska has 586,000 square miles of majestic beauty, over three million lakes, and more active glaciers than any other region on the globe.

But there are few people and fewer roads—*no* connecting roads in the western half of the state, only the empty promises of dirt trails leading a few miles out from villages to nowhere. And Alaska is truly a "poisoned paradise." It can thrill you and it can kill you. If the cold, the ice, the grizzlies, the wild seas, the mountains, the loneliness, the wolves, the prices, the snow, the sourdoughs, or the five thousand earthquakes per year don't kill you, the 586 billion bat-sized mosquitoes will! All I mean to say is, this is untamed country.

We finally ended up in a small homemade log cabin in Cooper's Landing, a rural village on Kenai Lake, population ninety-nine—counting the dogs. There were a few Alaskan natives, but most of the people came from other places, especially from the "Lower 48," to get away.

There is a religion in Alaska, and it goes something like this: "Leave me alone!" When we arrived, Alaska was, and still is, filled with quite a collection of loners, people who don't look kindly on interference of any kind, each with his or her own set of quirks. And everyone carries a gun. So in 1957 no one wanted a missionary knocking, asking them to go to church. (That was probably *why* they carried guns!)

One of our quirky neighbors (a "neighbor" in Alaska is anyone within twenty miles) would eat only meat, and he especially loved venison. He had no dental or personal hygiene, so his gums became blue and very swollen, and one by one his teeth began to rot and fall out. He became very depressed and despondent and would not even let our concerned missionary mother visit him in his cabin.

Weeks later, my older brother, Greg, and I encountered him while we were hunting. We were ten and twelve at the time. When he grinned at us, we were amazed to see that he now had rows of teeth in his mouth. I asked him how in the world he suddenly had teeth. "Simple," he said. "I shot a small male deer and pulled his teeth with my pliers and stuck 'em up here in my bleedin' gums. Hurt like the dickens, but they took root! Now I can chew as good as anything."

My brother and I stood stock-still on that snowy trail, staring in amazement. Then my brother asked, "Do you ever have any problems with the teeth?"

Our neighbor winked, shot us another big sourdough grin, and said, "Yeah, I now have BUCK teeth!"

When we got back to the cabin, Mom and Dad listened intently to our fascinating story.

We didn't see the twinkle in their eyes.

The Guide Bug

Since we had nothing, surviving off the land was a matter of necessity. Mom dug a garden in the nearly frozen soil during the short summer season and grew vegetables. We scraped for bullets and hooks, then hunted and fished for meat. We tried to stay warm by layering used clothing sent by concerned relatives. (It was so cold that we lined the seat in our outhouse with Styrofoam or old magazines so our butts wouldn't freeze when we sat down.) After a hunt, we'd carry the bulky, unevenly cut, bloody moose quarters on our backs through barely passable backwoods, using light backpacks not designed for large game, tied haphazardly and hanging much too low. Moose blood, mingled with our own sweat, trickled down our necks and bodies and onto our clothes as we staggered through muskeg, a boggy area with decayed leaves and peat moss. Black flies, moose flies, and mosquitoes attacked and bit mercilessly. Bears and wolves, never very far away, smelled blood in the air. The raw meat was unbearably heavy, but carrying a rifle along with the packs, which often weighed as much as we did—or more—was not optional. Sometimes we would trip and fall forward, the full force of the meat driving our faces brutally into the ground. It hurt desperately, and it was almost impossible to get up by ourselves if we were packing alone. But somehow we got through these hunting trips. Dad's way of hunting wasn't pretty, but I was learning how to survive through grime, grit, and guts.

Our big vacation (pronounced *Hunting and Fishing Trip*) each year was to the Tangle Lakes off Denali Highway near Mount Denali, known outside of Alaska as Mount McKinley. For a while we used the same tent we had used on the Alcan Highway. Later a church gave Dad an ancient little camper in place of speaking fees. Wow, what comfort! Well, for Mom, Dad, and our sister at least. My brothers and I slept in the leaky tent. We fished for grayling and huge lake trout and hunted for caribou. We ate blueberries, moss berries, and cranberries; swam and washed in cold remote lakes; and fished from dawn till dark to get some of our winter meat supply. Repellent was expensive, hard to find on the road, and therefore a rarity. Mosquitoes and no-see-ums ate us alive.

Dad taught us the nuances of fishing streams and lakes. My brothers listened carefully, but I had different ideas. There is room for creativity in almost any adventure. I would walk out into the middle of the stream in my leaky hip boots, throw directly upriver, and reel like crazy. I caught a ton of fish, and no one could believe it, but actually, *landing* them was the hard part in the fast current!

Even though these trips were in the heart of grizzly and wild-game country, Dad encouraged us to take small pup tents and hike as far into the hills and tundra as we dared and camp overnight by ourselves. My older brother went with me, and Dad allowed us to experience the real Alaska. We ate rhubarb, berries, and wild onions or cooked fish to stave off hunger. We also learned about special Alaskan herbs. This was an Alaskan gourmet guide school in progress. We were wild boys with big guns, but we still shivered at night in our tattered cotton sleeping bags when we heard the wolves howl over a kill. I was becoming addicted to living on the edge at a young age.

Our "luxurious" camper finally broke down for good. Dad had to leave his cherished camper at a nearby decrepit lodge owned by an old, grizzled hunting guide named Butcher. He was a big, rough man with a bushy, scraggly beard—the classic Alaskan sourdough— who thought the four major food groups were moose, caribou, beer, and squaw candy (which is salmon jerky). He often bragged about his "Alaskan seven-course meal," which was a six-pack and a can of Spam.

Butcher called himself a "master guide." But back then, a "master guide" was someone who could convince two people to hunt or fish with him. When Butcher told my dad that he needed to move the camper, they negotiated, and Dad swapped the camper for a hunting trip to the backwoods of Alaska. I was about to experience my first guided hunting trip.

At the time, Butcher was guiding some members of a famous family. I thought they were the richest people I had ever met. They paid a thousand dollars each to hunt. I was so impressed with their camp: big, comfortable whitewall tents; animals being caped, cut up, and packed; food cooked and served to all of us. Hunting to me had always been unplanned, inhumane, barbaric work, with long, heavy packs, messy carcasses, and cold, damp sleeping conditions—practically torture. But this was a different world, a world I instantly loved. That day I caught the guide bug, an adventure bug without a cure.

There was no trekking through frigid swamps here. My dad and

I left camp and were hauled in a "weasel," a converted military, all-terrain, tanklike vehicle. Butcher had installed a winch attached to a metal arm that would swing to load heavy items. He could easily winch the animals up on the weasel and pack them out. We drove back in the wilderness about eight miles from a dirt road over streams, swamps, alders, and small hills. I marveled at how easily we were able to travel over almost impassable land. The trip took about two hours. I kept thinking about how long it would have taken to walk or if it even would have been possible.

Killing a moose is like getting a year's worth of gift certificates at your favorite butcher shop, and our family needed the meat to survive. At the start of our hunt, we positioned ourselves on a hill overlooking a clearing. Nothing was happening, so Dad and I both fell fast asleep.

I was awakened shortly by a strange sensation. Suddenly I saw—less than fifty yards away—a big bull moose with huge antlers! My heart was racing. I gently eased over to Dad, who was on his back, and crawled on top of him. He opened his eyes and looked at me, quite startled. Our eyes were less than an inch apart. I could hardly speak but managed in a sputtered whisper, "Moose, Daddy! Moose, Daddy! Moose!"

"Where, Rocky? Where?" he whispered back.

I carefully pointed and tried to whisper, "There, Daddy. There, Daddy, there!" Can I shoot 'im, Daddy? Can I? Can I?"

Dad hesitated, then finally whispered, "All right, Rocky. Just don't gut shoot him."

I took my WWII vintage .303 rifle and blew that big moose down with one shot—right in the middle of his guts!

When we got to the animal, Dad looked at the gut-shot moose. He stood motionless for a moment, and my heart froze. He cut his eyes at me, and I stared back. I noticed a small grin begin to creep into his face, and he muttered, "Nice shot, Rocky." We both burst out laughing. What a great moment and what a gift. The antlers measured fifty-three inches, making it my second moose of this size during my teenage years.

Little did I know that our chance meeting with Old Man Butcher would set the tone for the rest of my life. I was hooked, and my destiny was starting to emerge. Like my father before me, I hunted and fished everywhere I lived, all through high school and every chance I could get while in college. And like my father, I kept hearing the "call of the wild" in my soul. I was struggling to find a way to blend this "call" with the "calling" to the ministry.

The Call of the Wild

After college, I married my lovely wife, Sharon, and attended Reformed Theological Seminary in Jackson, Mississippi. There I was given the nickname "Rockfish," and for good reason. If I missed some early morning classes, my professors would be much more understanding if they found cleaned fish, dressed wild turkey, or mouthwatering mallards ready for them when they got home.

After seminary, I was working in a church in California when a member invited me to go to a hunting/fishing show nearby. I gladly accepted and will never forget my amazement when I walked into the elaborate outdoor exposition and was greeted by hundreds of hunting and fishing booths, beautiful boats, all the latest outdoor technology, and thousands of people seeking adventures.

And then I saw the picture. I stood spellbound in the middle of the aisle because I recognized the little creek displayed in it. As a young boy, I lived in a roughly hewn log cabin next to that creek in Cooper's Landing, Alaska. I fished, waded, and drank from that creek! It was Cooper's Creek! I also saw pictures of the Kenai River, into which Cooper's Creek empties. I spent hours on its banks too, fishing, tossing rocks, and watching the wildlife.

I asked the owner of the booth about his operation. His chest swelled as he said, "Son, I can take you to places you have never been! The Kenai River is one of the foremost king salmon fishing rivers in the world, and you can fish it for only three hundred dollars a day!" I was thinking fast—three hundred a day! I was lucky to make that in a week! I could probably fish the Kenai River better than this guy could! I was sure of it.

I rushed home and excitedly told a very shocked Sharon, "Honey, I am going to be a fishing guide in Alaska!" She struggled to be positive, but I was sure the Lord would approve. After all, He'd be due at least thirty bucks a day!

With help from some dear friends, I began my quest. I had professional-looking brochures printed, conjured up a business name, and made big plans.

The first year all of eighteen people signed up. It looked as though the Lord was going to have to wait awhile for His money! But the next year there were thirty-six sign-ups. The following year there were sixty-four, and finally I was able to begin paying debts and dream of a future. Read on! As the man in the booth said, "Let me take you to places you have never been!"

TWO

Double Trouble

Early in my guiding career I teamed up with Ralph Meloon Jr., a fourth-generation Ski Nautique boat builder and fellow Alaskan adventurer. He is a pilot, and we decided to outfit and guide hunters and fishermen into remote Alaska. On this trip we were to fly supplies two hundred miles from Soldotna, a small town on the banks of the Kenai River. Soldotna was across Cook Inlet, far from civilization, to Red Devil, the site of an old mercury mine, long since abandoned. It is inaccessible by road but still boasts a usable gravel airstrip and a few die-hard Alaskan villagers. From there, I was to ferry a boatful of supplies through one hundred miles of remote rivers to a small wilderness upper river camp near the famed Taylor Mountains in southwestern Alaska. Ralph would use a Super Cub that we kept at Red Devil and ferry supplies by air to the camp as well. Ralph had earlier flown in our clients, a group of daredevils from Focus on the Family (go figure!) who had decided to experience wild Alaska. They wanted to do it all: hunt caribou, moose, grizzlies; and fish. We all got more than we bargained for.

Ralph's DeHaviland Beaver plane, the airborne SUV of the

Alaskan bush, is a real workhorse, unlike the Super Cub, which carries only the pilot and one or two passengers. The DeHaviland has a two-thousand-pound payload, and it was loaded to the gills with our survival gear. We had packed and fueled it up the night before for an early start. But inexplicably, the tail of our plane got moved during the night, and part of it was just behind a protective steel post. In the early darkness we did not realize it. Being in a hurry, we strapped ourselves into the plane and started to taxi off when—*crunch!*—the tail of the plane was damaged beyond immediate repair. Ralph looked at me and I at him. We were thinking the same thing: *We'll never make any money at this!* I hoped this wasn't an omen about our trip. Was someone trying to get our attention?

Down but not out, Ralph and I unloaded what gear we could into his Cessna P-210, which has a decent payload of almost fifteen hundred pounds, but it is much smaller volume-wise, so it is difficult to take advantage of the payload capabilities. We had to leave behind almost half of our supplies. Wham! What a tough way to start our new venture! I felt like Gideon when God took away most of his army. I prayed silently that the Focus on the Family group had an inside connection with the Big Pilot in the sky.

We flew to Red Devil, transferred the cargo to my boat, and many hours later finally made it to the upper-river camp. Everything was in order, and I began to relax. The "cook's tent" beckoned with the smell of food, the Cabela tents were up and outfitted with comfortable sleeping bags awaiting our tired bones, and the sound of group laughter was soothing and satisfying. Things were good.

Sleep was indeed nice, but dawn came all too soon. We arose to the chilling Alaskan cold, wolfed down breakfast, sipped hot coffee, and slipped into our boats. We "ran the river" by quietly drifting downstream and searching for game along the banks. This is a wonderful way to quietly sneak up on game. We did this for a couple of days and saw moose and bears but no caribou. We hunters have a saying "If you want to catch a trophy animal, just don't bring your gun," because what you are looking for is either never around when you want it or is everywhere but you can't get to it. On this trip, naturally, the primary animal sought was caribou, which was nowhere to be found.

After several days of running the river without success, Ralph scouted by air from the Cub, and voilà! He found several thousand caribou on the western ridges of Taylor Mountain. Now we were in business! Everyone was excited. In most places the rest would be easy. Pick up the hunters, land nearby, locate the herd, and get ready for fresh steak! Not here, though; this is wild, remote, untouched, untamed Alaska.

There are no landing strips or remote airports. So the gutsy Alaskan bush pilot depends on his ability to land a small plane modified with big soft tires, modified struts, and props. In addition to these modifications, he has to land on uneven, bumpy ridges that he has probably never seen before. He can only guess from the air if they are sufficient strips of land suitable not just for touchdown but for takeoff.

The Alaska bush plane has been tinkered with for at least seventy years, mostly from the Alaska Flying School of Hard Knocks. Larger, softer tires were designed that roll over rocks, tundra, frost heaves, rough terrain, and small bushes and alders. These "bush-wheels" are a great aid in landing on tight river sandbars and tricky mountain ridges. The landing gear is usually extended and beefed up, and oversize power propellers assist in getting airborne quickly. A STOL (short takeoff and landing) kit enables modifications to the wings and struts to promote maneuverability at low speeds and landing in tight spots. All excess weight has been removed, such as executive seats and fancy interiors, and thus a very effective "lean, mean hunting/fishing flying machine" is the result.

Even with all of these improvements, the Alaskan bush pilot must be keenly aware of the air currents, visibility, amount of weight he is carrying, and what time his sourdough wife said he should be home. Each landing and takeoff could be his last. Ralph is one of the best natural pilots in Alaska. He is a true adventurer and will take calculated safe risks so that he and his clients can experience great hunting in remote Alaska. But it's not a job for the faint of heart!

Ralph and I circled and looked for a safe landing area near the caribou. The pickings were slim. We decided on a narrow, hump-backed, sideways ridge on the western side of the Taylor Mountains. It was tricky, but the wind was good. The Cub carries only one passenger and light gear. Ralph nailed the landing and dropped me off. He quickly made six round-trips from the camp to the ridge, hauling the hunters and their gear, for a total of twelve landings. As he got ready to take off from the ridge for his trip home, he said to me, "See you in three days, Rocky. Have a great hunt!" Everything seemed perfect. Things were going so well it made me nervous. The excitement in the camp was high, and the men could hardly sleep.

The next day we awoke, began hunting, and were soon in caribou heaven. The men harvested five dandy animals. Their fun continued as they relaxed and chatted. I, on the other hand, was busier than a lady on a freeway headed to work with a cell phone, a makeup kit, a bagel, and a baby. I had to gut, clean, and skin all the caribou and help pack those five animals back to the ridge. A fully skinned and quartered caribou amounts to about 150 pounds of packable meat. Hunters who want to display their success and prowess usually want a mount of some sort (what is it about us men?). European mounts, which include the skull and antlers, are often enough. But some hunters love shoulder mounts or full mounts, which require the corresponding partial or complete cape packed out. A full cape is the complete skin or hide of the animal, which is skillfully removed and used to re-create a life-sized display.

Caping is to a guide as surgery is to a doctor. We carefully remove the hide from the shoulders, neck, and head of the animal. We use fairly small but very sharp, deeply curved knives, and it is a daunting and dangerous task that requires a lot of skill, but the resulting half (head and shoulder only) or full mounts are really worth it.

These caribou capes, along with the antlers, added another fifty to seventy pounds each. So we had over one thousand pounds to pack. Since we are in remote areas, we have to pack the meat all the way back to the bush plane landing area for it to be loaded and flown back to the lodge. So a good guide develops a knack for finding game close to the landing area! (A moose cape alone can easily weigh over two hundred pounds and is awkward to pack.)

My last pack was just before dark. I had long since run out of water. The lack of fluid and the strenuous exercise gave me the worst leg cramps I have ever had. I bent over in extreme agony. Since then, every time I see professional athletes get leg cramps and go down clenching their teeth, they get my full sympathy!

Ralph flew in early the next day and was desperate to get us, and the meat, off the ridge. A huge and deadly cyclone from Siberia was headed directly at us and could lock us down for days or weeks. It was to be one of the worst storms in years. Alaska always has bad storms, so the prediction that this storm was going to be *really* bad was significant, like saying it was going to be a *really* hot day in the Sahara—now, that would be a scorcher!

Ralph was delighted that we had caribou, three of which were bagged, tagged, and ready to be flown out. The other two had been packed but were not ready to be transported. Flying out the meat, cape, antlers, and gear is tricky. The weight must be distributed just so and the wind read properly for the plane to get airborne quickly with its load, all from a windy, rocky, bumpy, slanted ridge. Horns and rifles are often tied to the struts under the wings, affecting lift and maneuverability. The temptation is to carry extra weight so fewer trips can be made, but this can prove to be deadly.

Since weather changes quickly in Alaska, those left behind by a bush pilot require enough survival supplies for as many days as necessary for that plane to return or for other help to arrive. Water is especially critical, because much of Alaskan waters are contaminated by an intestinal parasite called *Giardia lamblia*, affectionately known as "beaver fever" because it is typically passed from the stool of beavers. (Note to novice hunters: Boiling water is the way to kill this little inconveniencing parasite.)

Guiding has reinforced the lesson that my teacher taught about government and the balance of power. This branch of government offsets that branch, just as a guide offsets a pilot. A good guide packs every inch of a plane and then finds a way to stuff in more. A good, prudent pilot is constantly, discreetly rearranging and lightening the load—and cursing out the guide under his breath. A good guide and a strong-willed pilot form a great team and normally find a way of balancing the proper amount of risk versus safety. The pilot, though, when push comes to shove, has the final say, rather like a mule and its rider. The rider has the final say, but the mule usually wins.

Ralph and I worked well together. He moved the four hunters back to the river camp while I got the rest of the meat, capes, and racks up to the loading area. Ralph flew load after load, and finally it was time for me to leave. The plane was pretty well maxed out, weightwise, with my large frame, the extra meat, and the last of the equipment. Just as Ralph lit up the plane, the wind shifted dangerously. It was one of those moments pilots experience daily in Alaska. You start assessing the details, calculating the risks, and analyzing all the little things—things that can go wrong quickly. In this case, our plane was loaded to the gills with cargo, and the inconsistent wind was altering the effectiveness of our propeller and our steering capability. The meat began to slide in the hull, and we almost stalled, the engine threatening with its misfired sputters. But Ralph was cool, and we moved forward with the plane slightly lifting off and touching down on our ridge runway as we gathered speed. I gritted my teeth and felt my sigh filter through them as we finally got off the ground. Ralph kept the plane airborne and got us safely off the ridge. Looking back, I marvel at how often bush pilots tempt fate. They are like a black widow's mate. They just keep going back and challenging the odds.

It was great to get back to the river camp. I quickly jumped out of the plane, but suddenly, and for reasons I still don't understand, I turned and gave Ralph my new Gore-Tex jacket for his flight back to get the last caribou. It was getting chilly and dark, and the wind was shifting like the moods of a gambler at a racetrack. I knew Ralph was a great pilot but wondered if the odds were beginning to work against him. I had a nagging sense of foreboding. I tried to shake it off by cleaning up in the river and preparing tasty fresh trout, salmon, and caribou steaks for my guests and myself.

Time flew by. Where was Ralph? Where was the plane? And *why* had I given him my jacket? It was getting darker, maybe too dark to fly. As the flames from the warm fire we had built rose bright and hot, my soul began to chill. Could Ralph fly in the dark, and if so, could he land on this small gravel bar? I grabbed a chain saw and began cutting trees and brush, lining the gravel bar, and setting them afire to illuminate the landing area for a pilot I feared would not be coming.

We had another plane on pontoons tucked away in a slough nearby. I rushed to use its radio and try to raise Ralph. My worst fears were confirmed. I could hear the emergency locator transmitter (ELT) from Ralph's plane emitting a stress signal. Then intense relief washed over me as I faintly heard Ralph's voice. It was weak, but he was alive! I could hear him, but his voice was too faint to make out the words. He had obviously crashed and was down but conscious and talking to a Korean pilot flying a commercial plane far overhead. The pilot spoke little or no English and was having difficulty understanding Ralph's efforts to tell him where he was. I could hear the Korean saying something that sounded like, "muxolux kweek, muxolux kweek." Suddenly Ralph's radio went dead, and I knew that the foreign pilot would not be able to get help to Ralph in time. My relief evaporated into the gathering wind. I felt helpless. A camp full of hunting clients, a pilot down, and a major-league storm headed our way. I wanted to close my eyes and wake up from this nightmare.

I tried to focus, to put together what I did know and devise a plan: I knew Ralph was down, probably badly injured, his radio likely damaged, and he was carrying a fresh caribou kill in grizzly bear country. He had a tattered tarp and my Gore-Tex jacket. What other supplies he had would be minimal. I did not know where he was, but I did know the approximate route he had taken. The winds were beginning to howl, the storm was moving in, and it was getting very dark. I prayed for wisdom and had a flash of divine inspiration. Instinctively I knew that Ralph must have crashed when he took off from that tricky ridge.

Although I didn't know it at the time, Ralph's situation was growing more dangerous by the minute. He had landed on the ridge and loaded the last caribou in the tail of the plane. He had tied the cape and antlers high on the struts under the left wing due to the way the wind was blowing. But as he began takeoff, the wind changed direction and was now coming hard from the right, forcing the lighter right wing up, leaving the heavier left wing dragging. He tried desperately to correct but ran out of right wing aileron, causing the plane to lose lift and power. He crashed hard down the slope of the hill, crumpling and severing a wing, breaking off the landing gear, shattering the skylight and windshield, and mangling the prop and the struts. He had injured his leg and his arm and was bleeding from a gash on his head. He was disoriented and had few resources and little hope.

He knew it would be difficult enough finding him in daylight, impossible in the dark. His radio was transmitting poorly, and the winds and rain were rapidly increasing. Gusts of wind from the approaching storm had built up to one hundred miles per hour and were rolling the pieces left of his plane, over and over, down the mountain. Ralph curled up in his tarp and tried to gain footing on the cold, slippery slope. Against his best efforts, the wind kept pushing him toward a steep precipice further down the hill. He was beginning to freeze from the cold rain and the wind chill. The longer the wind kept blowing, the shorter his odds were of survival.

Without knowing why, I knew what I had to do. I asked the men in the camp to pray. I would leave immediately by boat and hurry back one hundred river miles to Red Devil for help. One man offered to go with me, and I gladly accepted. This is a tough trip by day and simply a nightmare by night. It would take at least eight hours and a minimum of forty gallons of gas to keep the motor fueled. And I was running low on energy and needed refueling too.

We loaded the gas; grabbed some coffee, jerky, and survival gear; and headed out. I was exhausted from the last two days of hunting and packing, and now I was on a rocky, turbulent river in the middle of the night trying to go a hundred miles for help. And to top it off, as we started, the wind *really* began to blow, and so help me God, the strangest thing happened: the force of the wind split a large spruce tree on the riverbank, and it came plunging into the river right behind our boat, causing a huge splash. As I watched the tree slowly tip and then forcefully smash into the river, I remember thinking, *Is this real?*

The debris in the river became a major obstacle to the propeller and operation of the motor. The flying branches and leaves from the wind caused us to question our safety and the success of our journey. The rain began to pelt down mercilessly, and the wind blew the boat all over the water. I struggled to keep the boat in the deepest part of the current to avoid rocks, floating logs, islands in the river, and low branches near the banks. Our feeble flashlight soon went out, and I had to traverse this treacherous river by the flickering stars and moonlight that barely came through. I concentrated on the only thing I could scarcely make out, and that was the winding shoreline. I was winding too—winding *down*—but I knew if I failed to get help, Ralph would probably die.

Hours went by of bumping into unknown objects and hanging on to the boat gunnels for dear life in the freezing rain. Suddenly the boat went airborne, and we crashed onto an island in the middle of the river. I realized I had hit a couple of partially submerged logs, which had functioned as a ski ramp, launching us onto the island. No matter how hard we tried, we couldn't get the boat free. It was wedged between logs and mud. Finally, we gave up, curled up in the bottom of the boat, and slept fitfully in the rain and wind. I despaired of getting help for Ralph.

At early light, I stirred and felt the boat rocking and wiggling free. The torrential rain had caused the water to rise rapidly in the river, lifting our vessel and setting us free. We bailed out the boat, freed the prop and motor of debris, got it started, and were relieved to continue our journey. We could now see, capitalized on this, and made good time, reaching Red Devil by ten o'clock that morning. We located the only establishment in town, a rustic grocery/supply/restaurant/hardware store. The owner went by the name Dangerous Dan. The sign on the door read, "Enter here if you wish me well, the rest of you can go to . . ." All I can say is, we were thankful he wished *us* well and even loaned us his plane to get help to our friend. Soon we were on the way to Ralph. It was not a plane that could land in the bush, but we hoped to spot Ralph and at least air-drop some emergency supplies to him.

The storm abated enough for us to fly all the way to the ridge. My premonition had been right: we saw the horrible evidence of Ralph's crash but were thrilled to see him waving at us and signaling that he was OK. We couldn't land but were able to make a drop of supplies close enough for Ralph to reach. Ralph had survived a crash and one terrible night. He had managed to fight the wind and rain and claw a foothold in the hill. I hoped he would make it until we could get another plane in there that could land and fly him out. And the odds of that would be slim if the wind did not stay down. Ralph was cold and scared but had new supplies and hope, knowing we would be back and hoping it would be soon.

He had bled on his clothes, and his blood was mingled with that of the caribou he had loaded the day before. A bloody, injured animal is a beacon in the wild. The bleeding caribou he had tied to the plane was less than a hundred yards away, still lashed to parts of the shattered aircraft. Ralph felt like a juicy worm dangling from a hook with hungry bass nearby. He told us later that as we flew out of sight, the hair on his neck began to rise; that was when he spotted the three grizzlies. He hoped they had not spotted him.

Ralph carefully covered himself with the ragged tarp and flattened himself on the ground. He prayed the grizzlies would go for the caribou meat and not opt for dessert. The bears sniffed the air and began to amble in his direction. Ralph remained motionless. The meat was behind him and a little to the side of the three hungry beasts. They stopped and sniffed again, seeking the source of their next meal. Closer and closer they came, and Ralph was afraid to breathe. When the grizzlies got to within twenty-five yards, his heart was pounding so hard he thought surely it would give him away. Then one of the bears seemed to look right at him and began to walk his way.

Ralph was now so tense and stiff he could not even blink. The other two bears continued to saunter toward the caribou meat. But the last bear stopped and gazed for a long moment right at Ralph. It was a moment he will never forget. Time stood still. His soul seemed to merge with the soul of the bear.

Finally, the bear broke the spell. He sniffed, shook his head a couple of times, turned, and trotted off toward his companions. Ralph suddenly needed to breathe. He gasped large gulps of air. He had no idea how long he had been holding his breath.

The grizzlies seemed to be quite content with the large, tender chunks of skinned and boned caribou meat. They ate for a while and then strolled off into the bushes. Ralph was glad they were satisfied, and his concerns turned to the weather. If it turned bad, no one would be able to come back for him the next day. He did have emergency medical supplies, a tarp, some more clothing, food, and the sure knowledge that we would do all we could to get him to a hospital. As the darkness gathered on the hillside, Ralph gathered up his courage and prayed for flyable weather. He also prayed the grizzlies would not be hungry again anytime soon and kept a sharp lookout in the direction he had seen them go.

The night was long and very cold. It was a good thing Ralph had received the emergency drop. The cold helped to somewhat numb his injuries, but his head began to throb, and Ralph knew he could not last many more nights without help. In the early morning hours he listened for the wind. Silence in this case was truly golden. Without wind he had been able to get a good purchase on the hillside and felt secure that he would not slide. As light approached, however, he began to hear the wind's rustling as it started to whistle in the trees. He hoped his rescue party had gotten an early start to beat the ongoing buildup of the wind. Suddenly, hope began to creep into his heart. He could hear the hum of a plane's engine! He recognized the sound as coming from a small bush plane, exactly the type that would be coming for him!

The hum of the tiny engine drifted in and out, but Ralph was sure it was headed toward him. Intently he watched the skyline, and then he saw it! At first it was a small dot just above the ridge, moving in and out of the clouds. But soon it grew bigger and bigger. The plane was indeed coming for him, and he almost shouted for joy when he saw the familiar waggle of the wings by the daring pilot sent to rescue him. He waved back and was greeted by another even bigger friendly waggle!

The pilot made a wonderful landing and carefully managed to get Ralph and his supplies into the plane. There was no time to delay, as the wind was increasing to a dangerous level, so the pilot taxied into position and took off into the ever-shifting, buffeting wind. It was perhaps not the smoothest takeoff, but it sure was the prettiest one Ralph had experienced in a long time!

We greeted Ralph with great happiness upon his arrival. I would have given him a bear hug, but I didn't want to cause more pain. This experience created a deep bond between us. Ralph knew that I had his back, and I had done all I could to ensure his safe return. This is a common phrase in many circles, but in the Alaskan wild it has a unique practical significance that wears down our foolish sense of self-sufficiency and compels us to rely on people other than ourselves. That is a great thing between men and not easily accomplished.

Ralph recovered physically, but I believe that an intense adventure such as this can often heal us in other, psychological ways, far better than pills or therapy. Somehow it rebuilds you in the same way muscle rebuilds—only after being broken down. Both Ralph and I had faced challenging odds, possible loss of life, and yet, when we discuss it, we agree that this incident made us feel very alive—and like he-men. We discovered a hidden part of our souls by nearly crossing the threshold of our bodies' limits.

THREE

Wolves in the Night

I don't provide alcohol at my lodge, but if someone brings in his own, I figure it is none of my business as long as he drinks and acts responsibly. Besides, I've never wanted to be Elliot Ness— Superman maybe, but not Elliot. I had one fisherman who came to the lodge and, on his very first night, sat at the table and set up three drinks. Let's just call him Hank. Hank-Who-Drank. Well, Hank put one drink in front of him, one across the table, and one next to him. He tipped his head slightly, grabbed the drink next to him, and downed it first. He did the same with the one across the table and then drank the one in front of him. I was a little intrigued about this routine of his but didn't inquire, and he offered no explanation.

The next night Hank went through the same odd process. I hadn't figured it out, but I held my tongue and let it pass. I mulled it over a couple of times the next day but couldn't come up with a plausible explanation. This happened again the third night, and by then I was flat-out puzzled. I *had* to know.

On the fourth night my new friend set out only two drinks. He omitted the one in front of him. What was this? I watched as he went through an abbreviated routine of the earlier nights, downing only the two drinks. OK, that was it! What was going on?

I gave him a wry smile and said, "Hank, you've got me baffled. You drank three drinks each of the first three nights you were here, going through a rather strange routine in the process, and then, all of a sudden, tonight you only drink two. What's the deal?"

He gave me a surprised look, squinched his eyebrows a bit, and replied, "Well, I set one drink out for my honey, even though we divorced years ago, and I set out one for my daughter, who is married and lives in Africa, and I set out one drink for myself. Being a gentleman, I let my honey drink first, my daughter drink second, and then I finish off my own drink." He stopped. I waited, but he did not continue.

Finally, I broke the silence. "But Hank, why did you only have *two* drinks tonight? You didn't put one in front of yourself."

He looked at me, took a deep breath, drew himself up, and said, "Well, Rocky, it should be obvious! *I* quit drinking!"

Over the years I have learned that I probably discover more about my clients in one week than many folks learn about them their whole lives. A week in close proximity with someone while living great adventures brings out things both revealing and remarkable. People share their hearts, make vows of all kinds, and discover things in themselves that they didn't even know were there.

I was preparing for a late-fall, "hard horn" caribou hunt with two good friends. The later the season, the more likely a caribou or moose is to have rubbed the now-itching velvet off his horns. The velvet is the conduit through which the blood is circulated to the exterior "bone." Horns are a living part of the animal and necessary for defense from predators, fighting other bulls, and foraging in the snow, and they are great for intimidation.

These animals grow new horns every year, because once the velvet is rubbed off, the horns begin to die slowly since there is no longer a blood supply to them. Eventually they are shed in late fall or early winter. Horns losing their velvet are referred to as "hard horns." Next time you see mounted antlers, look closely and see if they are just the bare horns or if they have the velvet look. Both displays are quite beautiful.

A late-fall hunt is an easier hunt because bulls are in rut and, in a word, distracted! Love is like that, fellas! Rutting bulls are much easier to stalk. It is often still a very tough hunt, though, because of the weather. Winter descends on Alaska with fury and can be deadly, like a spider zooming across its web after a trapped fly.

Late fall is also absolutely the most beautiful time of year in Alaska, in my opinion. The bright colors of the foliage contrasted with the deep blue skies, and pure white snow creeping down the mountainsides are spectacular.

The hunt is basically a race against the creeping white "terminal dust" inching down the mountains and the freezing cold that follows. The animals hang out right at the snow line, and I, along with Mark Lang, my pilot, had spotted a nice herd of caribou on the edge of this winter forerunner, at about the thirty-five-hundred-foot level, in the Bonanza Hills near Mosquito Creek.

We had trouble finding a place to land but finally located a ridge, and Mark kept "dragging" it with his wheels. This is a dangerous method bush pilots use to try to determine the contour and obstacles of a particular strip of untested ground on which they want to land. It is similar to a "touch-and-go" in which the pilot almost stalls the plane and barely brushes the ground with his wheels. He then guns it and rolls lightly along the terrain, trying to "feel" the surface. Mark was finally satisfied, and we were able to land safely.

Mark Lang is an outstanding bush pilot and willing to take "sensible" risks when necessary. He said to me, "Rock, you know what the definition of the best bush pilot in Alaska is, don't you?"

"Sure," I replied, "the pilot who can take off or land ten feet shorter than the last guy!"

Mark nodded and said, "Well, be careful what some of these hunters tell you."

"Why would you say that, Mark?" I asked.

He paused, exhaled, and said, "I flew a couple of moose hunters from Alabama into a remote lake not far from here. They had a good hunt and both managed to get a large moose. When I returned for them, I told them I couldn't take them, their equipment, and the moose in one load because we wouldn't be able to clear the trees at the end of the lake. One of the hunters yelled at me, 'That's baloney! You're just chicken. We came out here last year and got two moose, and that pilot had a lot more guts than you. He took off, and his plane wasn't any bigger than yours!' Well, that ticked me off, and I told them if another pilot could do it, so could I. So I loaded up, taxied at full throttle—and dang if that plane didn't almost make it— but we didn't quite clear the last of the trees. We clipped the tops and flipped sideways into the marsh. I was hurt but alive, but I was real dazed. I shook my head, trying to clear the fog, looked around, saw one of the passengers, and blurted out, 'Where are we?' He looked out of the busted window for a moment, then at me, and said, 'I'd say . . . about three hundred yards further than last year!'"

Hey, you have to have a sense of humor in my business.

Later, Mark and I were setting up our tent when I looked up the hill about two hundred yards away and witnessed two grizzlies mauling a caribou. I looked at Mark and he looked at me. "I think we better move the camp!" I said, and we quickly moved the tent several hundred yards farther away from the grizzlies and tucked it into some alders on the hillside for protection from the wind. It was a bumpy patch of ground, but security is more important than comfort!

It was beginning to snow, and Mark said, "Rock, I can't use skis because I'm taking off of a gravel strip back at the lodge, so you'll have to keep the landing area tamped down if you want me to land. These soft tires won't work in soft snow. I'll need at least sixty yards of length and about eight yards of width." Snow has little definition from the sky, so we marked the touchdown area with an *X* made of game bags and each side of the "strip" with poles tied off using orange tape. Mark examined the entire landing area carefully before leaving.

Mark entered the location in his GPS, took off, and later returned with my two hunters, Steve and Dean Doerksen. Dean is a California entrepreneur, a successful almond broker, and very involved in his local church. Steve runs a horse ranch for his brother and teaches at a California high school. They were pretty excited, but I could see a little "environmental shock" when they arrived at the tent. Californians!

The next morning we woke to find that it had snowed about a foot during the night. This made walking and hunting laborious, and though we saw plenty of caribou, by the time we reached them, they were long gone. The ironic thing is that caribou usually reappear right where you were just hiking from! This is a phenomenon often reported by caribou hunters.

A friend of mine once hiked two miles from camp and eventually harvested a medium-size caribou. It was a grueling two-mile pack back. When he arrived, there were about seventy caribou standing around his tent, including many trophy animals! The surrounding caribou didn't even bother to move when he returned. How did *they* know he already had his tag filled and could not shoot them?

They just did. Uncanny! It's just like us men to spend all our time and energy searching around for a trophy, something to prove ourselves. Sometimes, though, in that search we sacrifice the bounty we have at home where (hopefully it's not too late once we figure it out) we find the real trophy, a precious wife and family who have been there all along.

Back to the Californians . . . We were skunked that day, but it was exhilarating to be out in the remote wilds of Alaska in the mountains. We were tired, and that night we all slept soundly in spite of the bumpy ground. It was getting pretty cold, though, and our drinking water was turning to ice. I put some in a bottle and slept with it to keep it from freezing. We learn many such tricks to survive in the Alaskan chill!

The next morning we couldn't even start up the propane stove because the connections had frozen. It had also snowed a couple more inches during the night. I was beginning to feel the pressure.

We started out and soon spotted a nice herd of caribou. After fruitlessly tracking them, I looked back toward our camp. I wasn't going to be fooled again! Sure enough, I saw a cluster of caribou, and we started after them. We got to within about two hundred yards of a terrific bull uphill from us, standing sideways and outlined against the white snow. What a perfect opportunity! It was Dean's turn, and he quietly chambered a round and took careful aim. *Boom!*

What? I saw snow fly up forty yards past the caribou! *Boom!* Another puff of snow, twenty-five yards in front of the caribou! I cracked up. I think the caribou was amused too! He just stood there looking at the snow where the bullets had struck. I started laughing so hard that I fell to my knees. Where *was* Dean aiming?

The caribou then bolted along the ridge, angling away and uphill from us, and on a dead run. Caribou can really move when they are frightened, and maybe my laughter frightened him even more. Dean was following the fleeing animal with his rifle, planning to shoot again, but I knew *that* was useless! Until . . .

Boom! I'll be tarred and feathered if that caribou didn't flip completely over and die on the spot! This time Dean had made the perfect shot right in the neck, killing the caribou instantly. It was one of the most amazing shots I have ever seen. And after seeing the first two shots, it was more than amazing—it was unbelievable! For some reason this really tickled me. Two of the worst shots I had ever seen followed by one of the absolute greatest! But, like all warriors returning from battle, Dean and I only brag about that third shot to this day. It was indeed memorable, and to top it off, this beautiful caribou scored well in the record books.

Hunting in big rugged areas usually involves a lot of sneaking up onto ridges, quietly getting comfortable, and using binoculars to "glass" (view) the whole area, looking for animal-specific color or movement, and then, once game is located, planning the best way to stalk them. I began glassing the area with my Zeiss binoculars and saw a huge caribou in a valley about a thousand yards farther down the hill. Good binoculars are a must for guides. Skill with them will allow you to find animals others would miss and save time you might have wasted chasing short racks. This one was no short rack! I looked at Steve and said, "Let's go!" Dean stayed behind to begin the tough job of packing his fresh kill.

As we carefully worked our way closer to the second caribou, I was more and more impressed with the size of his antlers. They were simply massive, and he was the king of his domain. He had a group of lady "bous" around him, and he was aggressively beating back any attempts from younger bulls to encroach on his territory. What a tough way to keep your lady friends.

Earlier in the day, Steve had complained about not feeling well, but during our stalk he was very excited and seemed to be fine. We got to within five hundred yards and began crawling slowly forward on our hands and knees, using clumps of snow-covered grass and tundra for cover. It took awhile, but this fella was worth it. He was a beauty, and fortunately for us, he was preoccupied with his harem.

As we got closer, Steve said to me, "Rock, don't help me with this caribou. I don't want you to shoot!"

I said, "OK, buddy, you got it." I hoped he would not miss, because this was a real gem, one of the biggest I had seen in a long time. I told him, "Steve, that rack is gonna look great on the wall at the ranch!"

Soon we ran out of cover and could not get any closer than 180 yards. I said, "This is about as close as we're gonna get. Think you can handle it from here?"

"No problem," Steve replied. "Now, remember, Rock, I don't want you to shoot!" I held up my hands and shrugged. I never had any intention of shooting. It was all about Steve. But I sure hoped he could bag this big bou!

There were about fifteen cows and a couple of younger males with the bull. Suddenly he approached one of the cows and mounted her. Needless to say, he was very preoccupied. I was thinking, *Whoa! What a way to go!* I could see a big grin on Steve's face. He was aiming carefully. Then I got to thinking, what if Steve hits the cow, or worse, kills both of them with one shot? *Well, officer . . . ah . . . this bull was doing his thing, and the bullet went through him and into her and got 'em both!* Yeah, right! Who will believe that one? Steve had only one caribou tag, and big-game violations in Alaska are treated extremely seriously in the state legislation and are aggressively enforced on the local level.

Since the bull was on top, Steve felt that the lower he got, the better chance he had of hitting just the bull. I hoped he was right. *Boom!* The bull fell sideways off the cow and went down—but he didn't stay down! Amazingly, the cow appeared puzzled but did not move away. I then watched in fascination as that huge bull staggered to his feet and stood on three legs. Steve had hit him in the right front leg, and the shot had come perilously close to hitting the cow! And then, one of the weirdest things I have ever observed occurred. That bull stumbled right back over to the cow and, somehow, mounted her again! That gal must have been something special! I do know that bull was really focused. Talk about not getting sidetracked!

Boom! This time the bull went down for good, shot straight through the heart. I am convinced, though, that he died with a smile on his face.

As we approached the bull, those horns just kept looking bigger and bigger. Although there are twenty-seven steps and criteria for scoring caribou antlers, with the most important factors being symmetry and mass, I knew this one would pass muster. It easily scored as a trophy rack, amassing 392 points SCI (Safari Club International). And, yep, it does look terrific on Steve's wall!

I suddenly realized it was getting too late to pack the animal out, and it would be a real job anyway due to the distance and his size. I quickly gutted it and moved the gut sack away from the caribou so predators would go for it and leave the meat alone. Steve and I then hustled back to the camp.

At first he was real excited about his kill, but after the work started and during the hike back, he began complaining about being nauseated and sick.

Back at camp we met up with Dean, and he was thrilled that his brother had scored such a nice animal. The weather was starting to get blustery and really cold. Steve didn't even want to eat. We gave him candy and a sandwich, and he went straight to bed. Fortunately, I had brought double sleeping bags and air pads for all of us. This kept us off the cold floor, and the two sleeping bags each kept us comfy and warm. As any camper in predator country knows, no food can be kept inside; we keep our food sealed in a plastic cooler, well away from the tent.

I dreaded the upcoming caping and packing of the bull the next morning. Skinning a fresh kill is much easier because the heat from the animal keeps your hands warm and the cape pliable. A frozen one is a different story. It is slow, tedious, freezing, dangerous work. Dean had not been able to pack out his caribou completely, so we had some tough work ahead. And now Steve was complaining about being sick! I must say, to me this illness seemed fortuitously coincidental and I was not a happy camper. I don't think Dean was either.

The next morning dawned cold and windy. I estimated the temperature at about ten to twenty degrees below zero, figuring in the wind chill. And as I had anticipated, Steve was bundled up in his sleeping bag and complaining that he could not help. I looked at Dean and shrugged. He looked at me quizzically saying nothing. Maybe he knew something I didn't. I was suspicious that Steve was dodging work but kept quiet. Well, the work still needed to be done, so we set off.

I began the tough job of caping and processing the frozen carcass of Steve's caribou. My fingers were getting so cold that they began to lose feeling. In this condition, I could cut myself and not even know it. It had happened before, so I took special care not to repeat this painful memory. I succeeded with fingers still intact and then sectioned the caribou in preparation to pack it out to the landing zone. I then lashed up one portion to my backpack, loaded up, and headed back. Dean was amazing. He finished packing out his caribou and then assisted me with Steve's.

At midday Dean and I returned to the tent for lunch. Upon arrival, we were startled to see that Steve's legs were protruding outside of the tent, toes up! Not only that, but he was shoeless and his socks sagged down, leaving his lower legs bare. Snow had partially covered his feet and legs, indicating that they had been exposed to the freezing weather for some time. Was he dead? I saw no movement and got no response when I called out to him. Dean and I rushed to the tent, and I shook Steve.

"Steve!" I yelled. "Are you okay?" I was relieved when I got a response—weak, muffled, and unintelligible, but a response nonetheless. Steve was alive!

I pulled him into the tent and got him back in his sleeping bag. "Steve," I said, "you can't sleep with your feet outside the tent! You'll freeze!"

"I need to go home," he mumbled. It was then that I realized Steve had not been faking. The man was seriously ill. We needed to get him out, pronto!

We resumed our packing with a sense of urgency. We got most of the meat packed out and then heard the plane buzzing overhead.

But Mark couldn't land because the landing area was full of fluffy snow. He flew down below the snow line, found another landing place, and waited. Dean and I began tamping out the runway. This involved stepping side to side and mashing down the snow with our feet so the plane could land on the packed snow. It is tedious work and reminded me of my childhood dance class: *Slide, step, step. Slide, step, step. Turn and step!* Do you know how long it takes to tamp down a sixty-by-eight-yard strip of snow a foot deep? That's right. Six days. Well, not really, but it felt that way, and when Dean and I finished our masterpiece, we were exhausted.

The plane returned and landed safely. Dean assisted Steve to the plane while I loaded up some of the caribou. Steve was then flown immediately to the lodge to receive the help he needed.

Afterward, Mark returned for Dean, but by then it was getting late. When Dean left with more of the meat, I knew it was too late for Mark to fly back for me. He would come for me and the last of the meat the next day. It sounded like a good plan at the time.

I was tired, and it was freezing, so I ate some cold grub and hit the sack. I wasn't going to let bad weather, aching muscles, and chilly vittles disturb my rest. Nothing did at first. I was out like a broken bulb when suddenly something startled me. What had I heard? Then I heard it again. Something was outside my tent! I kept hearing heavy breathing and occasionally a faint brush against the tent. Was I imagining it? Nope, I was wide awake. I heard it again. I thought, *Must be one—or both—of those grizzlies I saw the other day. What should I do?*

I got my rifle, chambered a round, and placed it next to me, barrel pointing toward the tent door. Now, of course, if a big ol' bear attacks me, he will surely use the door, right?

I chuckle at how we expect animals to behave as we do. I have seen the silhouettes of grizzlies from inside my tent before. None have ever attacked me through a tent wall. Of course, this can and does happen. I learned later that a lady was killed in her tent when a grizzly bit her head *through* the canvas. And a friend of mine had to shoot through the canvas at a grizzly that was shredding his tent while he was inside. Bears have an excellent sense of smell and can easily tell where your head is by locating the smell of your breath.

I reflected on another time when I had a knife but no gun and knew a grizzly was in the area near my camp. I cut a stout piece of alder, sharpened one end, and placed the butt portion in the ground next to me in my tent. I figured if the grizzly charged me, I would hold the butt end fast into the ground, angle the pointed end at him, and using his momentum, pierce him with the stick. Thankfully, I did not have to test this idea, but the next morning I discovered the grizzly had left his calling card—a big blueberry pie, four inches from my tent!

In spite of the noise outside my tent this time, I felt reasonably safe and finally drifted back to sleep. Isn't it odd how soft covers make us feel safe in our beds and the thin walls of a tent give us a sense of security? It is really an illusion, like some of the other silly things we trust to protect us in life. We think our wealth will protect us from tragedy, our fatherly threats from daughters' boyfriends, or our dusty Bible from God's loving intrusion in our lives.

The next morning dawned, and I awoke, proud that I had been able to sleep in spite of my nighttime visitors. I exited the tent and stretched my stiff muscles, and then I saw them. Tracks! Dozens! These were not grizzly tracks; they were wolf tracks. It had snowed a couple of inches overnight, and I could tell these were very fresh. There was even a well-worn trail circling my tent. There were also numerous snow-beds (snow-padded areas formed where the wolves curled up and slept) and a significant amount of wolf urine. It was easy to see that not just a few animals had been present. Why had they visited my tent? Wolves had never surrounded my tent before—a grizzly or two, maybe, but never a pack of wolves.

I was still thinking about this while on my way to pack out the rest of Steve's caribou. I had just come into view of the kill site when I stopped dead in my tracks! Voraciously eating the remains of the caribou were fifteen wolves! My nightly visitors in person! I sat down, retrieved my binoculars, and began watching them. Then I saw something really odd: a little red barrel-chested domestic dog was with the pack. He was about as unwolflike as you can imagine, obviously deemed the runt and treated like one. He brought up the rear and ate last, but still, here he was, trying to fit in, running around with his short, puny tail sticking straight up! I immediately felt a kindred spirit with this spunky red rascal who was tackling the odds and finding a way to survive.

I had heard that wolves usually run when humans approach. I decided to test this theory, because I could see that a good portion of the caribou was still edible. I got up, started making loud noises, and moved toward the wolves. Sure enough, they dispersed, and I hastily packed up the salvageable portions of meat. Then I beat a quick retreat back to camp.

I fully expected the plane to come and get me, but as darkness descended, enveloping the day, gloom flooded me, and I knew I was destined to spend another night with my newfound canine friends. I immediately removed all foodstuffs from the tent. I was still wearing bloody clothing but had nothing else to put on. With two sleeping bags wrapped around me, I hoped the scent would be muffled and minimal at best. Why were the wolves around my tent, anyway? Go howl at the moon!

Did wolves attack people? I wondered. I had rarely heard of unprovoked attacks but did vaguely recall some chilling stories by Jack London concerning wolves. I knew they attacked dogs (well, not lil' red ones, but all others). But people? Hmm, I wasn't sure, but I wasn't going to take any chances! I loaded my rifle and my .44 Magnum handgun and laid them, plus two sharp hunting knives, next to my sleeping bag. If those wolves attacked, they were in for a surprise. I would be ready. I was determined to take out at least two or three of them.

After zipping up my tent (tight!), I checked my weapons and tried to go to bed. But my mind was racing. Would they come back? At first I couldn't get to sleep, but when all continued to be quiet, I drifted into a sound slumber.

Sometime in the middle of the night, I awoke to the terrifying sound of an adult wolf howling over a kill. I sat bolt upright, motionless, straining to hear anything. There! The brushing noises again! I could hear the quiet patter of feet and an occasional low growl close to the tent. As my ears adjusted to the nocturnal noises, I could distinguish the differing panting sounds. The wolves were here again! *What should I do?* I thought frantically. What *could* I do?

I don't know which is worse, a close brush with death or being in limbo, in a powerless, helpless position where you have no control over your fate. The latter, I think.

I sat motionless for a long time, perplexed on how to proceed. Then I got annoyed. For courage, I said to myself that famous Italian quote: "Fuhgedaboutit! I'm going to sleep!" And I did. I won't lie though; I did wake up once or twice!

Morning found me still safely tucked in my two sleeping bags. I looked at the tent walls and saw no holes or tears. So I got up, unzipped the tent a small crack, and peeked out. No wolves. I stepped outside and looked around. All clear. But it had snowed again, and I could see that a new and deeper trail had been tramped down around my tent. There were new snow-beds and lots of urine markings, some on the snow-covered alders right next to the tent. They were getting bolder and I didn't want to stay another night and see how bold they would get.

I rushed to begin the laborious task of tamping down the runway, a requirement due to the fresh snow, and patiently (albeit anxiously) waited for the beautiful sound of my bush plane. Ah! There it was! I had not been forgotten. Bad weather near our lodge had kept my plane grounded the day before. But now, with better weather Mark was able to return. He flew me, the rest of the caribou, and all the equipment back to the lodge. And what a difference! I left a snowy, cold, blustery, wolf-infested mountainside to arrive at a lodge that was warm and bright—and there were no wolves! (Well, not the four-legged kind, anyway.)

I was relieved to learn that Steve was doing well. Then I got Dean aside and told him about the wolves on the mountain. We both mused over the fact that the wolves had come to my tent when I was alone. I have often reflected on that and wondered how my four-legged friends sensed that I was by myself, knew that I was vulnerable. In life, I have discovered the same. People who want to advance their agenda any way they can come after us with sharp teeth, always seeming to know when we are vulnerable. The bulwark of close companionship and support of real friends is a critical part of my life. Through this experience I developed a deep and lasting relationship with my two new trophy friends. Steve's caribou antlers scored very high in both Boone and Crockett and the Safari Club Gold Records, but the greatest thing achieved on this trip for all of us was true friendship. An adventure like ours can bond you to other thrill seekers for life. If you walk into Steve's house today, his favorite picture is not of the caribou, but of the three of us, grinning stupidly and huddled together in the Alaskan snow.

FOUR

Dances with Bears

Two fine Southern gentlemen, Rhett Madison and George "Bubba" Dixon, were on their way to Alaska to hunt with me. Rhett had made his stake in the cotton industry and was one of the biggest operators in the rich Delta region of the Mississippi River in the state by the same name. Both men were classic, refined gents from the Deep South, which meant they loved their "shootin' and their scotch."

Rhett closely resembled Colonel Sanders both in appearance and age and made quite an impression with his snow-white hair and beard. He had a shooting range on his cotton plantation and was a skilled marksman. Bubba was also familiar with his rifle and hunted frequently. It is unusual for busy professionals in corporate America to find time for this declining art, so it was a pleasure to have someone who knew how to handle his weapon safely and could hit what he aimed at.

Conversely, my average client is middle-aged or older, over-worked, out of shape, and as nervous as a third grader en route to the principal's office. Naturally, we in the guide business understand this and are familiar with "buck fever." Buck fever has nothing to do with making a dollar but everything to do with making the shot! Some of my clients freeze up like a soon-to-be-father when informed his wife is in labor. We realize instinctively that we need to back up these "courageous warriors" and discreetly assist in harvesting a "wounded" animal. Good guides take all necessary steps to ensure a wounded animal does not suffer needlessly. I was delighted to have a couple of gents on this trip who would likely not need to be "backed-up."

I had been flown in earlier to prepare the drop-off camp, and the only landing site I could find was more rugged than I would have liked. The pilot and I landed, and a rock hit the rear landing wheel and tore it off. We checked it out and, with typical Alaskan can-do attitudes, fashioned a short stick from an alder, sharpening the tip and forging it into place so it would hold the plane's rear off the ground. This caused its profile to resemble a giant mosquito. After that I went about setting up camp in anticipation for my guests. It was a bright, sunny day, and from our overlook we could already see caribou milling about in the distance.

My new tent had a notice on the package that promised it could withstand winds up to seventy miles per hour. I barely took note of this because there was little wind, and I positioned the tent in a good, comfortable spot on the side of the ridge. I looked down the mountainside and saw that the only freshwater source was a small creek quite a ways down through rough terrain. I made a mental note to conserve the five gallons we had for the whole camp.

Our makeshift repairs on the plane seemed to work, and we were able to take off without a hitch.

We flew the Mississippi boys in, and I was tickled to hunt with a couple of homeboys, as my family roots are from the Deep South. We had a nice meal, chewed the fat, and slept in anticipation of the morning hunt.

We woke up to a thick, splotchy fog that made visibility sporadic. We drank hot coffee and kept our eyes peeled on the patches of hillsides that we could see. I spotted some nice caribou about a half mile off and said to Rhett, "Let's go get 'em!" Off we went. But we could only get to within about three hundred yards downhill from the caribou, which presented a difficult shot. One was a particularly gorgeous bull with pretty markings. Rhett got down, carefully took aim, and knocked down that beautiful animal with one incredible shot. We finished the climb to the caribou and took a couple of pictures. All the while Rhett had a very satisfied look on his face. Then he smiled at me and said, "Well, Rock, guess I'll mosey back to the tent and have a lil' drink." I grinned and agreed and set about processing the caribou. When I finished, I headed back to the tent for a short break.

Let's just say I found Bubba and Rhett in wonderful states of mind and obviously intoxicated . . . on the beautiful scenery all about us. Wanting Bubba alert, I fixed a quick meal and talked him into going on a short hunt, hoping to get him a caribou before dark. Fortunately, we only had to walk over a couple of ridges, and bingo! We spotted a beautiful bull caribou. Bubba rushed his first shot and missed but gathered his senses and made a crack shot on his second effort, bagging the caribou cleanly. But even with Bubba's help, it was still getting close to dark when I finished packing it to the camp.

I was a tired and bloody mess, having dealt with two caribou on the side of the mountain. I was parched rotten for a drink of water. But when I reached for the water jug, I was astounded to find that the five gallons I had left in the camp were all gone. There was not even enough to boil up some Top Ramen or soup or chili beans, all common fare at drop camps. My one daily hot meal was supper and usually consisted of precooked fresh fish or caribou and some type of hot soup, chili, or noodles. A hot meal and a warm sleeping bag at night energized me for the whole day. But now there was no water. Nothing to make my hot meal with! *Rhett must have taken a bath in it!* I thought. He didn't seem to be concerned either. He saw me looking longingly at the five-gallon can and ruefully at the creek far below.

"Rocky," he said, "we need some water, son. I need it to cut my scotch!" I nearly hit him. I tried vainly to smile and managed to say with some effort, "I'll be glad to fetch that water, Rhett."

Still smarting, I set down my cherished .338 rifle, a gift from my long-suffering wife, and strapped on a still-quite-bloody backpack, which had been used all day to haul caribou meat. I asked Rhett to put the five-gallon container in the pack. He obliged and said, "You be careful, son." I mumbled a reply and started down the mountain.

Someone once said, "When emotions climb high, wits run low." A quarter mile down, I realized a part of me was gone. My emotions *had* dulled my wits, and I had forgotten my rifle. I was too tired and embarrassed to go all the way back to retrieve it, so I pushed onward in my quest for water. Now, when a guide doesn't have his gun, it is like a piece of him is missing. A guide may forget to eat, forget what day it is, forget Valentine's Day, forget he is married, but he *never* forgets his gun.

The terrain was open in some places, but I had to traverse a number of ravines that contained alders. Alders are God's way of playing Pick-Up Sticks in the Far North. They grow together in a tangled mass, are eight to twelve feet high, and average about an inch in diameter, with leafy green foliage. Northern animals use alders as Southern animals use bramble bushes and briar patches: for refuge and ambush points. They are certainly a favorite hiding and attacking place for black bears and grizzlies.

My clothes and my backpack were blood-soaked and smelly from the caribou, and bears have a very keen sense of smell. They can sniff a mosquito burp at fifty paces. Their favorite meal is caribou, and here I was soaked with caribou blood and, hence, a virtual walking grizzly buffet. The sky was getting darker, and my mood was getting darker with it. I began to hear every noise in the woods, and each one sounded increasingly like a heavy animal stalking me. I tried to shake off my fears and told myself I was imagining things, and I finally reached the creek without incident and began to fill the water container. But my fear was growing and energizing me. I knew I would return up the mountain faster than I had come down!

Suddenly I felt a presence near me. I knew without a doubt I was not alone. It was the same feeling I had gotten in a dark room or garage when I knew someone or something was in the dark with me. Those who have experienced this know the exact feeling I am describing. My ears twitched, my scalp tingled, the hairs on my arms and neck rose, and all five senses came acutely alive. I don't recall hearing anything specific or seeing anything unusual, but I believe that man has senses he rarely taps into that often flare to life in times of acute fear or stress. I strained to see, smell, or hear what was there, without success, but I still knew something was wrong.

I quickly finished filling the container and put it into my pack, then started back up the bank. Curiously, my previously aching legs and back no longer hurt.

Crack! I heard the sharp snap of an alder off to my right. I hustled up the bank through an alder patch and headed for a large clearing. When I got into this open meadow, I began to relax and feel safer. A bear has poor eyesight, but in the open, one could certainly tell I was not a caribou, or so I hoped. My pack now weighed about forty-five pounds, so I concentrated on a good solid pace to get me back to camp.

Then the weirdest thing happened. I realized later it was divine intervention. Seemingly without reason, the strap under my right arm came loose, causing the backpack to become unbalanced. My nerves were already unbalanced.

I did not want to stop and make a full repair of my pack, so I simply bent over and began tying together the loose pieces. In this bent-over position, I could see behind me. It was then that I saw a huge, brown, massive flash. It was a grizzly bear, barreling across the meadow directly at me. I whirled around, facing him. Bears can move at amazing speeds for short distances, and he was about forty yards away and closing fast.

Intense adventures often have one or two moments of pure clarity. The complex becomes simple. It is life or death. I knew this bear thought I was a caribou. And I had witnessed two grizzlies the year before charging a young bull caribou in the snow. The caribou never had a chance. They were on him before he could flee. One hit him in the shoulder, and the other nailed his hind legs. The caribou went down so fast and hard it was unbelievable. The end was quick, and the grizzlies were feeding on his flesh in a New York minute. They had casually looked in my direction, with blood all over their faces, as if to say, "Unless you want to be next, you'd better steer clear."

My mind was filled with this and other thoughts as I faced the charging mass of muscle and fury. I had to convince him I was not a caribou! I thrust my arms forward with my palms open and fingers waving—the classic pose telling someone, or something, to halt!

I held my hands over my head with open palms. In a purely instinctual moment I started screaming in a high voice; it probably sounded like a teenage girl being chased by a monster in a

Halloween horror flick. At the top of my voice I screeched, "No, *no, no,* NO!!!"

Imagine the world's largest professional football linebacker coming at you at top speed, just about to hit you full blast and knock you into next week. I knew that not only was I going to be slammed with the force of a sledgehammer—and squashed flat—but that I was going to be chewed to a painful death.

Suddenly I remembered that my backpack extended above my shoulders, and the frame covered my neck. If I dropped on my stomach, curled up tightly, pulled my arms in, and lay still, maybe the bear would bite into the pack and water canister instead of my neck. If he rolled me over with his huge claws, though, I was a goner. Bears usually kill by going for the back of the head and end up biting the neck with their powerful jaws.

Many who have survived bear attacks have done so by lying motionless and letting the bear bite them. Often they get bit horrifically on the backside, but they just hunch up and hope the bear won't bite their necks. Using this technique, some have survived to tell their story. The bear tastes foreign meat, catches the human smell, and since he is not being attacked himself, quickly loses interest. Well, this bear had not lost interest and was almost upon me—much too fast for me to try my theory.

I am not sure *exactly* why, but the bear began to slow down. He may have been puzzled at the antics of this "caribou" hopping around and screaming like a mad banshee. Or he may have gotten a whiff of my *human* scent. (I don't know how, because he had charged me downwind.) Whatever the reason, when he got about four yards away, he came to a complete stop and reared on his hind legs, facing me.

What a magnificent bear! He was simply towering above me. He was probably nine feet tall and must have weighed between 650 and 700 pounds. He was a true interior grizzly bear, officially called a *Toklat*. These bears have dark brown legs and golden-blond backs. My vision was instantly clear, focused, and sharp, and I could see every detail of his large head and massive teeth.

I honestly did not know what to do, so I continued to hold out my palms toward him and scream, "NO, NO, NO! STOP! NO, NO! *STOP!*" The puzzled grizzly did not seem to know what to do either. He continued standing on his back legs but started shuffling side to side as he began to circle me. I shuffled with him and was surprised when, for a brief moment, I became aware of a full moon visible in the darkening sky just over his shoulder.

His eyes locked onto mine. They were intense and surreal, and I was transfixed. Time stood still as we continued our strange, almost hypnotic dance in the mystical moonlight. He suddenly startled me back to the present when he began snapping his jaws together, creating a loud clicking sound, *CLACK, CLACK, CLACK, CLACK*, in rapid succession. When bears clack their teeth, they are agitated, confused, and totally unpredictable. As he snapped his jaws, he also made a barklike growling sound. This was even worse.

We continued to circle each other cautiously, like two boxers in a ring. I was screaming like a stuck pig, and he was barking and growling like an angry dog. It sounded eerily similar to a bunch of seals and seagulls squawking over dead fish on the beach!

While he stalked me, he had gotten the stronger scent of the caribou blood, but probably not the full human scent. As he slowly circled me now, he finally got directly downwind and, for the first time, got *my* scent. He stopped and, just as casually as you please, gracefully dropped to all fours. I froze, waiting for him to make the call. He looked at me a few moments, a few that seemed like a lifetime, and then, as calmly as if he were strolling on a sunny beach, he slowly turned his huge, golden-blond back to me and walked away.

He knew that he did not have to hurry or fear me. He had won this round. I have to tell you that his big, beautiful rear end—*moving away from me*—was the most beautiful thing I have ever seen.

I don't remember the hike back to camp. My body and mind were shocked with the relief and adrenaline that had been surging through me.

"Rock, you're white as a ghost," Rhett said as I dumped my pack, sat down, and without prompting began reliving my encounter. I told them about my dance with the bear, and I couldn't stop talking and sharing the details. My heightened state propelled me, and I spoke rapidly, rushing my words. They intently listened, start to finish, their mouths gaping open the whole way through. They could hardly believe . . . nor could I, even now.

I had emotionally, physically, and mentally endured one of the most intense moments of my life. I knew that I had looked death in the face, and it stirred my heart. When I completed my story, I was emotionally charged but physically completely drained.

We stayed up talking a little while longer, my guests electrified by my moonlight dance with the bear. But, as they began to tire and I began to internally reflect on what had happened, I knew that I had not done anything special or clever and believed in my heart that God had intervened and saved my life. What a day! Now it was time to get some sleep, if I could.

We crawled into our sleeping bags, and during the night the winds blew fiercely, with gusts far exceeding seventy miles per hour. The entire set of poles in my beautiful new tent snapped, and it collapsed on us and began to slide down the slope. We had to fight to keep the tent from being blown over and down the mountain.

Later that night I was reminded of the two thieves on the cross, not because I was in a spiritual mood, but because of the effects of the frightening wind. One of my clients was cursing; the other was praying and making confessions and promises to God. (I won't get into those confessions, but I smile every time I think of them.) I silently sent up a couple myself, the encounter with the dancing bear still etched in my mind.

FIVE

Drifting into Death

To put it simply, bow hunters are a rare breed. They tap into a deeper level of noble, primitive instincts as easily as the rest of us turn on our faucets. They think, act, and feel differently than normal folks. Their elite view of their skills and artistry cause them to look with disdain on all other hunters. They are masters of the *real* craft of hunting! After all, they actually give the animals a sporting chance and must use more skill and wits than other types of hunters. If you don't believe me, spend a couple of memorable moments talking to one. Ask him about the "only way to hunt." Settle back and prepare to hear his "pearls of wisdom." Just don't say, "Why didn't you warn me?"

Bow hunters spend hours perfecting their craft. They have to, because they must get very close to an animal to be successful, usually 35 yards or less. John Hammonds, a rifle hunter, killed a caribou at 619 yards with a Browning 300 Short Mag, firing a 180-grain Winchester Supreme bullet. But compare that shot and stalk to a typical bow hunt. There is no contest as to which hunt is harder. The longest bow shot I've ever witnessed was by Gerald W.

Olson, an awesome bow hunter who was sponsored by Real-Tree. He shot a caribou with a Hoyt bow at 131 yards, an incredible, highly unusual shot.

Bow hunters are very patient and skilled at tracking and stalking. They often get only one chance to shoot, so they hone this skill. In my experience, muzzle gun and bow hunts are the toughest hunts. The big, wary trophy animals are difficult to harvest, and they clearly have the upper hand.

Some guides really enjoy the challenges that bow hunting provides. Bow hunts require extensive planning. First, the terrain must offer plenty of cover yet not be so dense as to hinder an arrow's path. It must also be accessible by foot and frequented by game.

Second, the bow hunter must carry both a bow and a heavy sidearm for safety if he is going to hunt the bigger animals, such as moose, caribou, and especially black or brown bears. (A charging moose or bear would be hard to stop with cannon fire, much less an arrow. It may die later, but *your* death may precede theirs.) Caribou are easier to harvest, due to their sheer numbers and migratory habits, but moose and bears, especially grizzly bears, are big and tough to kill.

I once watched a video of a bow hunter being charged by an angry ten-foot brown bear who was highly annoyed by the pinpricks of the hunter's arrows. At the last moment the bow hunter drew a .44 Magnum handgun and shot the bear point-blank just a couple of feet in front of him. The bear almost fell on him as it died. I hoped my bow hunter this week was a good shot. I didn't want to deal with a mad grizzly. But we were about to test our arrows against a beauty.

Grizzlies hibernate in winter and come out in early spring. (Sometimes they emerge several times before finally coming out for good, like hitting the ol' ten-day snooze button. Guess they find it hard to wake up too!) A grizzly's size is directly proportional to the length of hibernation but is also affected by its food supply. In other words, sleep less; eat more; get fatter! Coastal bears, especially in southeastern Alaska and the Kodiak areas, have a warmer climate, a longer eating season, and a shorter hibernation. Thus, these areas produce much bigger bears. So-called interior bears are smaller and usually meaner because they live in a colder climate, have less food, and hibernate longer. (Hmm. That's familiar: eat less; get cranky—sounds like a couple of diets I have tried!) Due to shortened summers and less sunshine, the interior (grizzly) is generally darker in color than its fair-weather brother. It is this dark-legged, blond-back, inland bear that is more aggressive and has been known to attack humans.

Actually, the two types of bear are essentially the same but live in differing climates. Yet one study in Yellowstone National Park listed twenty-six different classifications of bear. This study was later debunked.

One Alaskan definition indicates that fifty miles inland there is a line separating coastal (or brown) bears from grizzly bears (also called *Toklat* or *inland* bears). You may be surprised to learn that I have personally watched grizzly bears turn into brown bears right before my very eyes. I have even seen them *turn back* into grizzly bears! You can witness this phenomenon, too, by carefully traveling inland exactly fifty miles from the nearest coastline in Alaska. No doubt, the park rangers will be glad to assist. Simply chart the fifty-mile dividing line and watch the bears cross back and forth over it. It is truly amazing to watch their transformation!

Nonresidents of Alaska cannot hunt a grizzly without a guide. I knew that this trip with my nonresident client could be harrowing for all concerned. I have seen the smallest stick, limb, or large blade of grass deflect an arrow from its path. My client was from Florida and managed an insurance office. We'll call him Bart. Bart the upstart. A bow hunter *and* an insurance salesman! What was I getting into?

How can I explain hunters and their need to be listed in a trophy record book? Well, cannibals eat the hearts of their victims to steal their strength and to feel proud of their conquest. Hunters want to be listed in a record book showing they got the biggest animal. The bigger the animal harvested and the higher the hunter is listed, well, the bigger the man he must be.

"Bart" desperately wanted a trophy Toklat grizzly that would qualify for a Pope & Young Club listing.

A Pope & Young listing is the ultimate recognition for a bow hunter. To qualify, the bear cannot be shot at any time with a gun. Since few grizzlies are harvested by bow and arrow, a big one would likely get certified. Bart kept telling me, "Rocky, don't shoot 'im! *I* want that record. Don't shoot 'im! I *really* want that listing!" This went on for quite a while, and I was getting frustrated. But I just kept gritting my teeth and saying, "I'm *not* gonna shoot 'im, Bart, OK? I *won't shoot*." Meanwhile I'm thinking, *Yeah, right. That sucker charges me, all bets are off.*

I knew where some big grizzlies had been seen, so we headed toward a place called Kashegelok. We were hunting the river in the spring. The boat motor was purring, and the scenery was gorgeous, but Bart's mind was elsewhere. As we traveled 136 miles up this river, Bart must have said 136 times, "Don't shoot 'im, Rock! DON'T YOU SHOOT! I want that record!" I was at the breaking point. I decided that if he said it 137 times, I was going to shoot *him* and feed him to the very grizzlies he sought!

Springtime in Alaska is unique. There are twenty to twenty-two hours of daylight. Bears often sleep during midday and stay up and eat all night. (I have teenagers who do that too!) Also, as the rivers thaw or develop thin ice, various animals, when crossing (especially heavier ones, with hooves), break through, get trapped in the freezing water and slippery ice, and drown. Each spring, grizzlies, black bears, wolves, coyotes, eagles, foxes, birds, and other predators search riverbanks for these dead animals. One animal's mishap is another's gourmet meal, sort of like when someone loses his position in a company. You got it: a feeding frenzy ensues. I hoped I wasn't going to be some hungry grizzly's next meal.

We were still cruising upriver when I spotted a huge Toklat grizzly on a hill near the river. I expected the bear to turn and run or at least move away from us. No way. That bear gave us a good looking over and then started walking directly toward us. He continued down the riverbank and out onto a gravel bar. The muscles rippled beneath his fur as he strolled into the river. Steam rose from him, giving him a halo effect. Was he coming at us? He *was* beginning to paddle toward our boat with powerful strokes.

There is an Alaskan law against harassing any animal in water with a boat and motor, but this guy was harassing *us*. Didn't he know the law? There is also a law against shooting at game from a boat with the motor running. You must be drifting, without any power, in order to shoot. I moved the boat well upstream to allow the bear complete freedom to cross unhampered. Then I said to Bart, "Get ready." I knew that the best time to shoot would be after the bear crossed and was on the far bank.

I watched this powerful animal swim almost directly across this river as if the current did not exist, his forearms making huge swaths in the water. As he came parallel, he looked upstream at us and slapped his paw on the water in our direction! *This is not a happy bear*, I thought. Then he growled and slapped the water again! Oh boy. Suddenly Bart's arrows looked so tiny compared to even the bear's paw! I remember thinking, *I need a new career.* If this bear was that annoyed at a couple of boaters who weren't even bothering him, what would happen when Bart stuck him with one of those toothpicks? Yikes!

Again I moved the boat well upstream from where the bear was about to reach the bank, on the same side of the river. Then I yelled at Bart: "I'm going to time the current, shut off the motor, and we'll drift back near the bear once he gets out." Bart nodded vigorously, half-crouched in the bow of the boat. He was staring fixedly at the bear. His arms were tense, and he held the bow at the ready. The bear exited the river and paused for a moment, facing a five-foot embankment that hung out over the river's edge. Then he climbed up the bank with powerful clawing motions. Prior to turning off the motor and drifting back to the bear I had turned the boat so the bow was pointing at the riverbank. The boat's position was set, and I stood at the stern behind the wheel, one hand on it, the other on my rifle. Everything seemed perfect. But Alaska has a way of turning prudent risk into potential disaster.

The current caused us to drift sideways, back toward the bear! That's when I saw that the bear had stopped on the embankment. The bow of the boat, fourteen feet in front of me containing Bart and his arrows, was getting closer and closer to the bear. I had timed the river current perfectly, but I had not counted on the current taking us closer to the bank! The current nearest a riverbank is slower than the current farther out, sometimes even causing the water to swirl back and work upstream along the edges. I watched in horror as we slowly drifted right in front of where the bear had exited. Then I watched with greater horror as the boat's bow was pulled against the shoreline almost underneath the bear! An upstream eddy under the bank caused the boat to come to a standstill. We were sitting ducks! What had I done?

I saw Bart rise and take aim. His arm went back in a steady pull.

His body was rigid, and he was deep in a zone, looking intently at the back of the now slowly retreating bear. The bear was still only seven or eight yards away. If Bart missed and the bear turned on us, would the motor start on the first pull? Would we have time to get away? I hadn't even had my morning coffee! How did I go from safety to a death zone in seconds?

Well, he was never going to get a closer shot than this. He had better make it count! *Whoosh!* He fired, and I saw his arrow go through the back of the bear's neck and exit cleanly through the front. Too cleanly! Of all the places to shoot a nine-hundred-pound bear!

Bart was immediately exultant, thinking he had made the perfect shot. The bear wasn't even down and Bart was yelling, "I got 'im! He's a dead bear! I got 'im, Rock, I got 'im!"

Whoa! Was this a cartoon? *I* didn't see a dead bear.

I yelled, "Shoot 'im again, Bart! Shoot 'im! SHOOT 'IM!"

Bart screamed at me: "No, Rock, no! He's a *dead* bear. I got 'im! He's dead!"

Suddenly, this "dead" bear stopped, turned around, stepped back toward us, and reared up to his full height. He was standing and towering on the overhanging bank, directly over our boat! Was he going to jump in? *Hey, I've got no life jacket that'll fit you, pal!* This was way past serious. So once again I yelled, "Shoot 'im again, Bart! Shoot 'im!" Then, powerless to stop the words, I heard myself yell, "Bart, *shoot that dead bear!*"

Thus far I had been transfixed by this huge animal. When I looked for Bart, I was startled to see that he was crouched in a little ball in the front of the boat, right under that bear. *When did that happen? How did he get so small?* Well, this bear wasn't small—and he was royally ticked. Would the bank even hold him? I saw dirt and rocks falling into the bow from the underside of the bank.

I suddenly realized the bear was growling and roaring madly. I watched in terror as he started swinging his huge arms back and forth in front of him like a boxer, his giant claws looking like curved knives. His massive head swayed from side to side, and froth dripped from his mouth and large teeth, landing on Bart. I felt totally helpless, because Bart had drummed into my head—for the whole trip—that I was not to shoot. Was *that* why I didn't even think to grab my gun? Pope & Young, phooey! I had drifted straight into a death trap. How stupid was that? And I wasn't taking any action? What an idiot! What was this bear going to do? Would he jump into the boat? Would the impact crush us?

Most intense moments don't last long, but this one seemed frozen in time. The seconds dragged on. I had to do something! Bow hunters are convinced that if they make a good "stick," the animal will bleed out quickly and die. But I didn't see any blood on the bear, and if anybody was going to die, it was us. So once more I yelled at the human snowball in the bow of the boat, "Shoot 'im again, Bart! I said, shoot 'im!" And once again, between the bear's roars, I heard a squeaky little voice: "I got 'im, Rock. He's a dead bear! He's *dead*!"

I was dumbfounded. Was this a Floridian thing? Disneyworld–Animal Kingdom, maybe? Were these magic arrows? Did he see what *I* was seeing? Maybe I was dreaming.

RRRHHH!! The roaring of the bear brought me back to reality.

I couldn't help but admire the tremendous power the bear was displaying. He was probably over nine feet tall, and standing on that five-foot embankment, he looked like the biggest, tallest bear that ever lived. River water from his fur was being tossed in huge droplets into the air, some landing on me. Our eyes met, and I saw intense yellow light, like fire, burning in his eyes. His nose and mouth were belching huge volumes of steam and saliva. Yeah, he was some dead bear, all right.

Suddenly the back of the boat caught some current, shifted sharply, and struck a rock. The metal against rock produced a loud cracking sound, which startled the bear. He instantly stopped his growling and arm swinging. He was still shaking his head side to side, but much more slowly. It was decision time, now or never. In that split second I felt like I had hypersensory overload. I heard, smelled, and saw so many things in one instant: the water, rustling leaves, the current lapping the side of our boat, the heaving breaths of this enormous animal whose foaming mouth was reflecting bits of sunlight, and then—

Whack! The current slammed the boat into the rock again. Whoa! At the sound, the bear turned so fast that his feet sprayed us with dirt. He fled into the alders, and the crashing noise as he broke through the brush was incredible. He was mowing things down like a tank. I stood there, staring after him, holding nothing but sweat in my shaking hands and gratefulness in my heart. My legs turned rubbery, and I quickly sat down.

I looked at Bart, still rolled up like a day-old donut in the front of the bow. I said quietly but firmly, "Bart, he's gone." It was then that I noticed that Bart had another arrow already strung in his bow. He'd had it there the whole time! Maybe he just froze up and had been afraid to stand, since he was practically under the bear. Had he stood, the bear could have dropped to all fours and knocked his head off with one blow. Whatever the reason for Bart's failure, I guess I was willing to give him the benefit of the doubt. I said, "Bart, I gotta track that bear. You stuck him in the neck, and I need to make sure it isn't a serious wound."

I'll never forget Bart's next words: "He's a dead bear, Rock." I almost fell off the boat.

"Well," I said sarcastically, "I did what you asked, Bart. I didn't shoot him, so go ahead and notify Pope & Young!"

I beached the boat and began hunting for the arrow. I found it in almost pristine shape. It was covered with a small amount of blood and fur, but mostly I found fat on it. Just as I suspected: the arrow had not hit anything vital. (That's right, fat is *not* a vital organ, although I have tried to convince my doctor otherwise for years!) The bear had gotten stung but was not seriously hurt. He *was* seriously mad, though, and I now had to track him. It is our code. Our integrity and Alaskan law require that we *always* track a wounded animal, even if it is obvious the wound is not serious.

I asked Bart to come along and back me up, but he said, "Just wait here a few minutes, Rock . . ." Then he paused, opened his mouth, and was about to continue—but I knew what the rest of that sentence was going to be.

"Don't even say it!" I shouted. He clamped his mouth shut and didn't say another word. But he wouldn't come with me. *Wonderful! Another wounded-bear stalk in the deep brush and alders—by myself.* Gosh, why am I so addicted to these adventures? Why *do* we stay in some of the careers we do? *I need a new brain.* I frankly hoped this "dead" grizzly was smart enough to be long gone.

I tracked the faint trail of bear blood often on my hands and knees for about three hours and then lost all sign of him. The whole process only covered a couple hundred yards. I saw only minute amounts of blood here and there, no white on the blood or froth (indicative of a possible fatal lung shot) and nothing else to indicate a serious wound. A heavily injured bear will usually head for water or lie in wait to ambush. This bear had gone in a straight line uphill and away from water. I was satisfied he would live to tell his grandkids about the two idiots in the boat and how he had let them go with just a warning.

I don't fully know why I never lifted my gun. It didn't even occur to me. I think, standing in the unbridled presence of such a powerful animal, I became transfixed with awe. I felt like, if you can imagine, that I was looking at life unleashed, full of power, threats, and glory. I came away realizing that man, with all his technology, weaponry, guts, and skill, is still no match for the impressive and sometimes unpredictable power of nature. That mighty bear and that drifting current became the distant death knoll, and yet we were allowed to live. Though Bart nicked that bear, I know the bear will have a long life. I'm glad, too, that something so ferocious and untamed will be roaming the mountains and valleys of my wilderness home, a home that heals and a home I love.

Sometimes I reflect on why my life has been spared on more than one occasion. I come to the same conclusion that many others do when their lives are spared: their lives were given back to them to enable them to serve a higher purpose. Life itself becomes more precious, they say. I agree. With Bart and I, we came into this hunt trusting the skill, weaponry, and the elite artistry of the bow to protect us in the wild. We were shown our place.

Survivors can and do accomplish noble things, not only for themselves and their immediate families, but sometimes for humankind as a whole. Priorities readjust for the better. Core values of family, integrity, appreciation for our Creator, giving back to nature, helping the less fortunate, and instilling values in our youth become our new standard. I suppose we would all like these values to become our standard naturally, without the need for such intense emotional trauma to jolt us into motivation for change.

Some of us, though, apparently need a stronger jolt than others.

SIX

A Series of Unfortunate Events

In the wild, the slightest recklessness can lead to huge disaster. A twig snaps at the wrong moment, the wind shifts ever so slightly during a difficult takeoff, you forget your trusty knife or gun, or you forgo a layer of clothing. It's these small details that can sometimes determine living or dying. And yet the balance between prudence and risk makes a great hunter. Regardless of how balanced you may feel, hunters at my lodge have said for years that it only takes "a series of a few unfortunate events to do you in." That's the allure, or maybe it's the curse!

To some, adventure just comes naturally. It's the way they live! They give in to the exhilaration every time. And a great adventure in exploring, hunting, or fishing can bring you and your companions into a stronger bond. Doing something with others that you do not normally do causes you to cheer them on and experience a sense of awe together. So it was with my companions Mike Moore, Steve Jones, and their pastor friend, Brian Hewes.

Mike Moore is one of the men I admire most, a man who played professional baseball for a living from 1982 to 1995. He has been the MVP of the World Series for the Oakland A's and was the only American League pitcher to get a hit in World Series play. One time he struck out sixteen New York Yankees, and on another occasion he took a no-hitter into the ninth inning against the Milwaukee Brewers. Yet with all his great moments and publicity, he is just a down-to-earth, roll-up-your-sleeves, hardworking farm boy. Mike told me that he gives 100 percent every time he goes to the pitcher's mound. He says, "When I give 100 percent, I'm always happy with my performance, whether my team wins or loses." Little did we know that we would need that type of attitude on this Alaskan big-game hunt.

Steve Jones, another professional athlete (if you can call golfers "athletes") loves to hunt and fish. I still enjoy watching "Jonesy" on the golf channel. Just the other day, I saw him playing golf in the Bay Hill Invitational, wearing his camo hunting jacket and hat. Steve is noted for being a champion. His wins include the AT&T Pebble Beach National Pro-Am, the Bob Hope Chrysler Classic, the prestigious United States Open, the Canadian Open, and the Phoenix Open.

Steve is a wonderful athlete, and he is also deeply religious. "Sure," he says, "golf is just a game, but it's also my job. It's OK for golf to hold a position of importance in my life and to treat it seriously, but if that's what's driving my life, that's wrong. God needs to drive my life, not a golf game." Steve believes that God can use difficult and unwelcome events for good in our lives. We would need that perspective as these two friends, Mike and Steve, and their pastor, shared "a series of unfortunate events" with me.

It was hot. For late August in the middle of the Alaskan Range, it was hot. When we flew over the caribou herds, they would literally be compacted in tight knots. Sometimes there would be five hundred animals in a round "pod." Those on the outside would be circling around with their tongues out, bellowing, *Haaaawt . . . haaaawt . . . haaaawt!* (Experts say this is one way they alleviate the swarms of gnats, black flies, and mosquitoes that pester the caribou.)

A lot of my guided trips are like having a reunion with friends, not just taking clients or unfamiliar guests into the Alaskan wild. Both Mike and Steve had hunted and fished with me often. We spent a lot of time around the campfire, laughing and recalling stories of grizzly hunting, moose hunting, and other hair-raising adventures. And believe me, no one can tell a story like a professional athlete; they spend most of their time trash-talking their teammates! This was truly a group of wild men in a wild place looking for a wild adventure.

Before we left the comfort and security of the lodge, we went over everything we would need in the Alaskan wilderness. I made sure the tents, sleeping bags, pads, food, cooking stoves, water, and guns were all loaded into the Cessna 206. The 206 is the "utility" plane of Alaska, also known as the Super Skywagon. The 206 side door is actually a double door. The double doors give the aircraft an advantage when loading cargo. The planes we fly in Alaska are built for more performance, adventure, and fun. Great mechanics, great planes, and a great prayer life keep us in the air!

With the Super Cub loaded, I took off to find a good ridge for both planes to land on. To maximize chances for a successful hunt, the ridge would need to overlook good berry fields for bears. Alaskan wild berries are a wonderful addition to an excursion in the wilderness. I can't imagine sitting and scoping or glassing for animals without grabbing a handful of this "Alaskan candy." Humans and bears alike love the famous Alaskan blueberries. In fact, in August, bears' tongues, mouths, posteriors, and skin are blue, and often their meat tastes as though it has been marinated in blueberry syrup. When we finish skinning a bear, our hands are even stained dark blue. I enjoy blueberries, but when I'm thirsty, I prefer to grab handfuls of moss berries, which are extremely high in water content. These food and water resources can save your life. Cranberries, lingonberries, salmonberries, high and low bush currants, dark purple blackberries, and bright red raspberries supplement our supplies in the field. Our cook loves it when we bring back some of these, from which he bakes great pies and cobblers.

Our location would also need to be rich in lichen for caribou, because what berries are to bears, lichen is to caribou—they love the stuff! Caribou lichen, or reindeer moss, is formed from a relationship between an algae and a fungus. The algae provides food for the fungi, and the fungus provides a structure on which the algae lives.

By the time Steve, Mike, and Brian arrived for the hunt, the heat had caused the caribou to look for the cool breezes on the high ridges and hills around Butch and Finn Mountains by the Nushagak River. Caribou head for the valleys to get water in the early mornings and late evenings.

I had flown four hours in the 206 the day before the hunt, and I had seen something that I would never forget. My pilot and I were about eighty miles from my Holitna River lodge, and we had just flown over the Chukowan River. The fog and misty rain on the hills kept us flying very low as we approached the Kazik hills. On a steep bank around a tundra ridge, I saw something very massive and white. Was this an Alaskan yeti? No, but it was a huge Alaskan albino moose! I could not believe it. As it ran into the alders, I felt sorry for it. Seven months out of the year this moose had the perfect camouflage: snow. But in August there was no way for it to hide in the leaves and trees. It was like someone playing hide-and-seek in the dark with a lit flashlight. My pilot circled this unusual Alaskan anomaly to give me a better look. I relayed this incident to the guys at the camp, and we all took it as a good sign about our hunt.

First Unfortunate Event. Joel Natwick, my pilot, and I found the perfect ridge with about twelve hundred feet of fairly smooth tundra and gravel to land on. Well, almost perfect. I didn't see a river or creek nearby, but I was sure one couldn't be too far away. We landed and unloaded, and the four of us carried our camp to a sheltered ridge. I told the pilot, "Joel, please check on me in two days, and make sure you bring water. With the heavy load, I wasn't able to pack as much as I would have liked." Big mistake.

Second Unfortunate Event. As Joel taxied on the ridge and took off, I suddenly realized I had not unloaded my satellite phone from the plane. I had no way to call Joel from our base camp without the iridium phone. I hoped this oversight would not prove critical, and I did not mention it to the hunters. I was becoming a little undone by these oversights. Low on water *and* no phone!

What a comfortable camp, though! Later that evening, we went scouting along the ridgelines, looking out at vast meadows. We spotted two huge bull moose and saw grizzlies working the blueberry patches. We also spied two black bears, but strangely we saw no caribou. We went back to camp, enjoyed a candy bar and a cup of coffee, and went to bed.

Due to a law referred to as "fair chase," you cannot fly and shoot the same day in Alaska. Animals cannot hide effectively from planes. Spotting game and quickly dropping hunters off close to the animals gives hunters too much of an edge. In fact, planes cannot be legally used to show hunters where game is located on the same day the animal is harvested, and ground-to-air communication for this purpose is a big no-no. Therefore we camped and eagerly awaited the next day's hunt.

When we awoke, the heat from the previous day had caused a heavy fog to envelop us. We could not see at all.

I grabbed Brian, and we started up the mountain to get above the fog. We walked all morning and most of the afternoon. Man, was that preacher in good shape! We saw a few caribou on far-off ridges but could not work our way to them. I had a water bottle in my pack, and so did Brian, but by late afternoon they were empty and we were very thirsty. I felt a nagging unease, as this was becoming an unwelcome theme of our hunt.

As we made our way back to camp, we were both anticipating a good meal and a big drink of water. Upon arrival, I saw that Steve was cleaning something using water from the water bottle! A tingling chill went up my spine. There were four men in camp, and after surreptitiously checking, I discovered less than half a gallon of water left. How had this happened so quickly?

My attention was diverted when I looked over and saw, on an opposite ridge with a giant half-mile canyon between us, a beautiful bull caribou. Immediately Brian and I took off, but the late-evening shadows were playing a spoiling role in our ability to stalk and get this animal before dark. When we got on the next hill, the big bull was already working his way down the ridgeline about three hundred yards away. We would have maybe one opportunity before he disappeared in the canyon and heavy alders.

Brian realized the difficulty, distance, and skill this one chance would require. He said, "Rock, I need to use that special gun of yours!" Good call. I have a pre-'64 Winchester .338 with great optics. What a wonderful, clean shot Brian made. The caribou collapsed immediately. The hardest part was marking where it fell and finding the carcass in the increasing darkness. But we managed, and I was thrilled for Brian. We took a few pictures, but it was late and I was in a huge rush to gut, clean, and pack Brian's animal. How pleasantly surprised I was once I started on the caribou to hear the voices of Mike and Steve hollering out close by, "Where are you? Where are you? We're gonna help!" They both pulled out their knives to help skin and cape, all the while exclaiming what a beautiful trophy this was for their friend.

The four of us packed out the whole caribou in one long, dark, challenging effort. I was amazed when Steve grabbed two front quarters in his hands and packed the front shoulders all the way back to camp without a meat pack. All right, so golfers *are* athletes! The next year, though, he had a medical exemption from the PGA because of his arm, and I often wondered if possibly that night, in the dark alders of Alaska, he had permanently damaged his wrist.

I put the bagged and tagged caribou about two hundred yards from our tents in the landing area. We had some great grub, swapped tall tales, and settled in for some shut-eye. I still had *my* eye on the water bottle though. It was empty. The only water left in the whole camp was a little that I hid in my thermos because I could not imagine going through the next day without coffee. I figured my guests would understand—especially if they didn't find out!

The next morning I got up real early, before anyone else, and silently and quickly made myself a thermos of coffee. I hid the thermos from my friends just as Achan hid the Babylonian robes and gold from Moses. I hoped I wouldn't get caught, as he had!

Thankfully, though without water, we did have some milk, which we drank with our cereal for breakfast. Then I showed the hunters the necessary berries to eat that day for hydration and explained to them how moss berries, which are especially high in moisture, would keep them from cramping up as they walked and hunted in the lingering heat.

We were just putting our unwashed breakfast dishes away when over the ridge appeared the most beautiful bear you've ever seen— and that bear headed straight for the butchered caribou we had stacked on our makeshift landing strip.

Third (almost very) Unfortunate Event. Steve told Mike he wanted to kill that bear with Mike's .300 Winchester Mag, so Mike hastily grabbed some bullets and handed them and the gun to Steve. Steve had used this same gun to bring down a grizzly with me the year before and had a lot of confidence in the bull-nosed, straight-shooting .300 Winchester Mag.

But what was this? The bullets would not chamber! We worked desperately to get the shells in the gun, but they just wouldn't fit. Careful examination revealed that the bullets were for a .300 Weatherby, *not* a .300 Winchester! This is an easy but deadly mistake to make. I asked a munitions expert later to verify what I already suspected. "What would have happened if Steve had chambered one of those rounds?" Without any hesitation he said, "It would have exploded and blown off his head!"

By now the bear was pacing back and forth in front of our stacked meat. I did not want to lose this tasty caribou after all the hard work of packing and cleaning and was pleading with Steve to switch to my gun, which was loaded and ready to go. The bear was looking long and hard at us. He apparently didn't like what he saw and began edging toward the canyon. Steve finally agreed to use my gun, but by then the bear had slipped over the edge of the ravine and disappeared into the alders. We were so disappointed. What a gift we had missed. I was especially upset. There would have been no stalk, and the bear had been so close that, if harvested, the pack would have been almost nothing! Guides have a saying when such providence occurs: "No stalk, no pack!" Yep, we had let that bear get away. We all walked to where the bear had disappeared, sat down, and contemplated if and when he would come out of the alders. We sat looking and reflecting about the earlier choices that had been made—almost fatal ones, it turned out—but we were all wise enough to keep these thoughts to ourselves.

I noticed the guys were eating more and more moss berries because of the lack of water. Something would have to be done! Mike and I looked way down the canyon and saw what we thought was the outline of a creek. Far below, the alders were growing in a pattern that suggested a small stream. I have crossed hundreds of canyon creeks that drain the high ridges and mountains, and the water has been clear, cold, and incredibly good. It was a calculated risk. If we found no water, we would expend time and physical energy, using up our small reservoir of bodily fluids and leading to dehydration. By now all four of us were complaining of headaches, the first sign of dehydration.

Fourth Unfortunate Event. Mike and I grabbed the five-gallon container and headed down the ridge to the alder creek. We stopped, ate berries, and watched a grizzly above us do the same. At last we got to the outline of alders. I grew uneasy, though, because we could not hear the sound of running water, and as we parted the heavy brush, we saw why. The creek was bone-dry! So we began to walk in the dry creek bed, with the alders, sagebrush, and willows making a perfect tunnel around us. This is where bears travel and live. Completely covered by the canopy around them, these streambeds provide total privacy from prying eyes. They develop into great walking trails and places to ambush prey. This was bear heaven.

We found some large sharp-edged rocks and began digging in the gravel streambed. We could have been in the Sahara desert; there was no sign of moisture anywhere. We did see some big watermelon berries and picked handfuls in order to get ready for the climb back up the ridge and into camp.

Camp was a little subdued, especially after Mike and I returned with an empty water jug. I explained that Joel, our pilot, should be back later that day with more water, but I couldn't contact him and confirm because I hadn't remembered to grab the iridium satellite phone! Brian and Steve exchanged glances. The stress had just been ratcheted up big-time. They knew how hard this environment was to survive in when you *had* water! Now it was a poisoned paradise. Even though there was incredible beauty all around us, there was bitterness at not being able to get a drink. I gritted my teeth and thought, *This is all my fault! Guiding 101—Always have plenty of water! What an idiot!* I was putting my friends in grave danger.

We listened wistfully for the sound that is music to all remote Alaskan fly-out hunters: the whine of the bush plane's motor. Silence.

Sometimes sitting and waiting makes a man focus on his life and purpose. Me, I was praying for rain. I had often taken a canvas tarp, spread it out during a chilly Alaskan rainstorm, and collected ample water for my camp. Get the drainage right, and it is surprising how fast water accumulates. But neither the weather nor my pilot was listening; it was still and hot, without a cloud—or plane—in the sky.

Then, about three quarters of a mile away, over a ridge, appeared a magnificent bull caribou, causing us to momentarily forget about being dehydrated and thirsty. His hard-horn rack etched against the blue horizon made all of us gape in awe. Steve knew it was his turn and said excitedly, "Rock, let's go!" He added, "I want to take this one with my bow!" I was all for the going but not for the "bowing."

You see, I had hunted with Steve another time with his bow. I had watched in admiration as he inched up on a caribou and stuck him with a terrific forty-yard shot. He then crawled into the bushes and hid as the bou staggered and lay down. I watched and waited, but Steve had his head down and would not finish the bou. *What in the dickens is going on here?* I remember thinking.

Finally, Steve caught my eye and motioned for me to give the animal the coup de grace with my rifle. I quickly and gladly obliged, then asked him why he hadn't finished the animal with a second arrow. He told me that he never wanted any animal he stalked and shot with a bow to see him. I made a wry face and looked at Steve oddly; however, I noticed when we went to look at his caribou that there were tears in his eyes. It was something deep and connected between the taker and the giver. Steve noticed my quizzical look and explained, "The Creator has endowed us with the power to take a life. Taking a life makes me aware of my own mortality and the fact that someday I will die." Steve dipped his head a little, pursed his lips, and added quietly, "I feel that if the caribou sees me, he will know about this power." To some this may seem strange. It did to me, just a little. But before you judge, you have to imagine what the seemingly endless wilderness can do to a person used to houses and freeways and comforts. He makes a connection with Nature, which confronts his own humanness and draws him into a free place where he can acknowledge these quieter rhythms the cities usually drown out.

So now, a year later, off we went, me with my rifle and Steve with his bow. This caribou had completed his trip over the top of the ridge and was working his way into a ravine that resembled a huge bowl. That was good. The chances for a good stalk and ambush with an acceptable range for an arrow were increasing as the caribou committed himself to this alder and brush ravine.

Back at camp, up the hill from us, Mike sat in a chair positioned to watch hunter and hunted, with a perfect view overlooking this brushy-bottomed ravine containing the caribou. Prior to our stalk, he told us he would watch and give us the caribou's location as it moved. I did not know how handy and helpful that would be.

We lost sight of the caribou in the heavy foliage before we were even halfway there. Steve and I circled the rim of the canyon, checked the wind, and debated the quietest way to approach this trophy. We had last seen him about six hundred yards off, just before making our way down the ravine. Where was this big guy now? It was like finding "Waldo." We knew he must still be there but could not for the life of us spot him.

I turned my Zeiss binoculars toward Mike, seated in the camp chair about a half mile up. I chuckled as he made huge gestures with his shirt. He crumpled it in front of him and then made a big circle as if winding up for a pitch. Once a baseball player, always a baseball player, I guess. Steve and I discussed what his wild gyrations meant and finally decided he was trying to tell us the caribou was lying down somewhere directly beneath us.

We devised a plan. We would split up a hundred yards apart and ease slowly down into the canyon. In preparation, we quietly stripped off everything that would make noise: packs, loose gear, coats, extra arrows. We could not afford to spook that caribou in this deep brush. Caribou on high alert will spring away at the smallest sound and very likely "jump the arrow." Jumping the arrow is when the animal jumps or darts off just from the small noise of the arrow's release or the twang of the string. Caribou reflexes are so quick that they can often avoid being hit. Their reaction time is not as quick when they aren't nervous.

I looked at Steve, all stripped down, and couldn't resist whispering that the grizzlies in this valley preferred rich men because their meat was tender and soft. He grimaced and just shook his head.

If we did our stalk right, we could wind up very close to this huge caribou. I had been charged by grizzlies and even a couple of moose, but never by a caribou. This did not concern me, though. What concerned me was getting a good clean shot for Steve's arrow. Bow hunters know that the slightest contact with leaves, branches, or underbrush will change the velocity and true path of an arrow, sending it careening off in another direction. Consequently, bow hunters in thick brush and alders are at an extreme disadvantage. I prayed we would get close enough for an unobstructed release of the arrow without the alders coming into play and ruining Steve's shot.

The slight breeze, nice warm sunshine, and lots of time afforded us the perfect conditions to get Steve tight and close to the caribou. Before entering the heavy brush, I trained my binoculars back on Mike. He nodded and smiled. I knew then that we had taken the right steps in finding "Waldo." We circled slowly, working our way to the bottom of the canyon. Steve was directly across from me. He had put on his full camouflage, including his face.

From opposite sides we entered a small open meadow. In the middle was a clump of birch trees with high grass underneath. I checked our spotter again. Mike was going crazy, jumping up and down and pointing at his feet. Either he was doing the rattlesnake dance—and we don't have snakes in Alaska—or the caribou was underfoot. We were right on top of our target.

I examined the small stand of birch trees closely. A limb moved slowly. But that was no limb! It was the top of the caribou's rack, and it was massive. The caribou slowly turned his head toward

Steve. I waved frantically at him to get his attention and pointed to where the bou was hidden resting under the small birch trees. I stood frozen and got ready to witness the show!

I saw Steve notch an arrow and draw back on the string. He raised the bow and aimed carefully. Whoa! That arrow was pointed at *me*! Not directly, but pretty darn close! And I was on the opposite side of the caribou from Steve! If the arrow got deflected, I could be the last "cowboy" to die by one! This dawned on Steve too. He motioned me to move out of the way and then signaled for me to make a loud noise so the caribou would stand up. What? Make noise?

Steve and I were only about thirty or forty yards apart. He was mouthing something to me, and I was trying my best to lip-read. I realized that he was saying he would not "stick" a resting animal. This guy was a true outdoorsman!

I wasn't sure what to do. If I made too much noise, I would completely spook the animal, causing him to jump and race off so quickly that Steve wouldn't get a shot. I watched as Steve took aim and began a steady pull on the Hoyt 50# draw weight bow. Maybe he had changed his mind and was going to shoot. I waited and watched, but still no shot. Now Steve had the bow at the ready but was still waiting for me to rouse the animal.

Fifth Unfortunate Event. I was getting ready to oblige when suddenly the taut gut bow string snapped, causing a loud TWANG. The unleashed arrow tumbled harmlessly to the ground. The *twang* was so loud and distinct in the quiet afternoon that the caribou reacted instantly. It leaped to its feet, lowered its head, and charged away from Steve—and straight at me!

Wow! He was one huge caribou! I felt like a matador, minus the red cape. The caribou was bearing down on me and was only a few yards away. I was fixated on those huge horns coming straight at my chest. What I did next was purely instinct. I yelled, jumped to the side, and rolled hard on the ground. It felt as though I was moving in slow motion. I could clearly see the large antlers going by me. How the horns missed me, I don't know. I felt the rush of the animal and pounding of the hooves as they flew by. I spun my head around to see if he was going to charge again. He was mad and frightened, but I think he was more shocked than spooked. He stopped about forty yards away, eyes wild, shaking his head and enormous horns. Was he contemplating another charge?

Steve ran over to me, threw the bow down, and said, "Give me that dang gun!" Nice of him to check on my status, eh? He then made a good clean shot, and he had his trophy caribou—the one that almost had *me*!

It was very hard to clean, cape, and pack the caribou without any water, so we ate at least a gallon of berries, sucking and cherishing each drop of moisture. By nightfall we had our second caribou bagged, tagged, and on the runway. On our last long, bloody pack, I was hallucinating about our plane sitting on the runway with water! Where *was* my pilot?

Water is important in so many ways, and if you ever wondered how many, go without for a couple of days. We couldn't get our hands clean or the blood off our clothes. (We reeked of caribou blood, and I know each man in his tent that night was praying that the grizzlies we had seen all around us wouldn't be attracted to our party and want a personal dance.) Couldn't boil soup either. But mainly we couldn't quench the deep thirst felt by *every cell* in our bodies. (It makes me thirsty just writing about it.)

We did get a small drizzle about 10:00 p.m. You should have seen us scramble to catch as much water as we could with a tarp.

Thankfully, we were able to partially nurse our parched throats, clean up a little, and go to sleep.

I don't know which was worse, no morning coffee or no water. We *had* to get water that day. We were out of energy, and no one got up early. We had all hoped that the sound of the plane would wake us. Had we been forgotten? Had both of my planes been in an accident? Did anyone know where we were? Did anyone care?

I fixed pancakes with maple syrup and lots of blueberries. We thought of the phrase "Got milk?" and laughed. We didn't have any of that either.

What a great bunch of men I was with, no whining, finger-pointing, or bellyaching. We sat around the camp table that morning, talking of sports, families, life in general—anything but water!

Suddenly, we heard the sound we all wanted to hear. The still of the late-morning air was interrupted by the distant drone of an engine. We swapped feverish glances and hoped against hope that it was our pilot, our plane, our *water*. Then the plane appeared over the ridge and began the downwind leg to land. It was coming for us!

When it landed, it was immediately rushed by our whole group. The pilot looked at us in alarm as we charged the plane. We immediately grabbed the one-gallon water jugs and drank and drank and drank. I became almost sick and bloated, but I couldn't seem to get enough. Untimely bad weather and other pressing matters had prevented our water supply from being flown in earlier. Knowing we were probably out of water and unable to come himself, Joel had sent in another pilot. We didn't care how it got there. We just overdosed on the best drink we've ever had.

What happened next still makes my blood run cold. For some unknown reason—I think maybe logic checked out with dehydration—we all decided we wanted off that mountain. The stick-rudder pilot said, "No problem. I'm light on fuel, so let's load up."

I knew the 206 was an incredible plane, but I wasn't familiar with all its capabilities and specs and wasn't convinced this was a good idea, so I asked him several times, "Can this plane safely get off this ridge with five *big* grown men, two dead caribou, and our entire camp?"

"Sure," he replied. "I think so. Let's get her loaded." We filled her up with all the gear, and then the men got aboard. But I noticed our driver had started to pace as we finished loading the plane. He walked the entire length of the ridge and looked over the edge of the steep canyon. What was he doing that for? He was beginning to look nervous, and that began to scare me.

The tree/alder line was about one hundred very steep yards below the rim of our ridge. The wind was slight but definitely moving right at us, and it is paramount to take off into the wind. Alaskan bush pilots love windy days; the only thing they love more than windy days is *very* windy days. Wind direction is crucial in any takeoff.

We taxied back up the ridge as far as we could to get the maximum amount of runway. We would need every inch in order to attain speed and lift. It got really quiet in that plane. I think everyone was acutely aware of the risk. There were raised eyebrows and raised heart rates. Mike, the heaviest, was in the copilot seat. Steve and Brian were immediately behind the pilot and Mike. I was in the last seat in the back. Only my eyes and the top of my head showed because there was so much gear packed around me. I had a fleeting thought that this was probably a good thing, that all those sleeping bags, pads, empty containers, and other soft items would at least cushion the impact of a suddenly probable impending disaster. Funny, as I think back on it, no one spoke up. Not one man said, "Hey, maybe we shouldn't do this!" Was it a macho thing? No one wanted to show fear? Or were we totally committed to the takeoff and living on the edge?

Vroom! We were off, racing to our fate. There was no turning back, or turning around. There was only the chance of turning *over*, maybe in our graves.

Sixth Unfortunate Event. The plane hurtled down the ridge. The 300-horsepower tri-propeller was red-lined, pedal to the metal, and the gas throttle was being pushed through the firewall by a desperate pilot. The end of the ridge was just ahead, and we still did not have speed or lift. This wasn't good. It would take a miracle to get the plane in the air now, and I doubted God would provide one for fools. We went over the ridge, past the end of our crude runway, and the plane still did not lift. It was going straight down the side of the mountain, headed directly at the tree line! Within seconds alders and tree limbs exploded into the prop!

We were tearing down the hill at a deadly speed. We were not getting much lift, and we were hitting the tops of young alders and small trees. Our plane was being violently jostled back and forth with each tree we would scrape. Our gear was banging around the inside of the stuffed hull. A sense of fear and exhilaration was pulsating through the plane. We knew that if we hit anything solid, we were dead.

As the plane hit the tops of the alders and trees, shrubs and bushes broke off and lodged in the struts, wheels, and in the cowling behind the prop. For some reason, though, the prop remained intact and churning, and the plane did not turn over and crash. It just kept following the ridgeline down toward the canyon at the bottom. I have since gone back to that ridge and walked to where the plane went over the edge and followed its path down, and I think I figured out what happened on that fateful day. As I studied the trail of broken limbs and alders, I saw an unusual opening in the trees, a gap that created a small meadow on the side of the mountain. The plane was never going to achieve enough lift and should have crashed into the side of the canyon wall or flipped into the mountainside at eighty miles per hour. But when the plane reached this God-provided opening, we were no longer impeded by shrubs and trees. This alone enabled our plane to finally achieve enough speed and lifesaving lift. We missed the canyon floor by mere feet and powered away from the canyon walls and the mountain, back into the beautiful blue sky. To reproduce that sequence and live to tell about it would be against all odds. Incredibly, the prop and critical areas on the exterior of the plane escaped serious damage.

In the plane, we all realized that we had just avoided death. I heard five men collectively exhale. I believe that we cannot truly face life until we face the prospect of losing it. We gazed steadfastly at one another, firmly believing that God had miraculously intervened. My friends' faces said it all. When we landed at the lodge, Steve crawled out of the plane first and plucked tree branches and alders from our landing gear and cowling. He gave each one of us a branch and told us to keep it as a remembrance of our deliverance. He then got down on his knees, kissed the ground, and thanked God. We all followed suit. We also faithfully swore we would never push the envelope that far again.

Today we each have a piece of those branches at our homes. When I see my alder branch, I am always moved by it. God spared us, though we did not deserve it. I feel that we were given a new lease on life. It makes me remember that, when I've loaded myself down with too much—too much guilt, too much disobedience, too much bitterness—God lifts me up. All that weight makes my soul scrape bottom; I can't get enough lift, I can't pull myself out. But God, who is gracious, lifts us out of our descent and moves us beyond ourselves to a higher purpose.

SEVEN

What Do You Say When the President Breaks Your Pole?

I have heard a story about Jack Nicklaus who played golf with several different presidents. "You know what they all have in common?" he says. "Mulligans!" (A mulligan is when you mess up and take a free shot.) "How do you tell a president he can't have a mulligan?" asks Nicklaus. "You don't!" It was the same for me with President George Bush Sr.

Waiting for the arrival of President George Bush Sr. was the most difficult part of my next adventure. There is a saying, "*mise en place*" (everything in its place), that gourmet chefs use the world over before a night of serving a fabulous dinner begins. The entire kitchen is prepared and organized—dicing and slicing, whacking and stacking, hors d'oeurve plates, dinner plates, condiments—everything is in its place, and there's a place for everything. You don't have to go looking for an onion to slice up for French onion soup; that onion is already diced and in a container right where you can find it when you need it. *Mise en place* were the words for my lodge and my staff.

My cook, Jon Burrows, a recent graduate of Johnson & Wales College of Culinary Arts, was excitedly preparing meals fit for a president. This was a once-in-a-lifetime opportunity to say he had cooked for the president. And not *just* the president, but an impressive entourage of senators, governors, astronauts, and executives.

What would they think of this wild, remote Alaskan river? We had four boats ready. I had a twenty-two-foot-long riverboat with a 40-horsepower kicker, which I had scrubbed spotless. I had my newest fishing rods and reels, and my tackle box looked as if it was right off the floor of a Cabela's superstore.

I checked my shirt for coffee stains, hid my cigars, looked at everything we had done, and saw that it was good. We then began to search the bright blue early-morning skies for the president's plane. Finally, we heard and then saw two beautiful DeHaviland Beavers and a 206, all using floats, approaching the widest part of the river for a landing.

I had worked out with the pilots earlier exactly where the best approach, deepest channel, and fewest rocks would be for their landing. No one wanted a mishap with this group of dignitaries on board. The planes, the guides, the boats, *everything* was set so our nation's highest officer holder, the most powerful man on earth, could enjoy a day of restoration through recreation with me in the Alaskan wilderness.

All three skilled pilots set their planes down perfectly. Their pontoons sliced through the clear Alaskan river heading directly for our planned rendezvous.

I was sweating bullets. What if I couldn't get a fish for the president? What if I turned the boat over? What if I accidentally called him George? What if he did not enjoy our adventure? Would *he* give *me* a mulligan?

The planes all beached in a slough right off the river. I knew which plane the president was on, and before the prop stopped turning, I was standing in the water by the floats of the 206 to meet and greet him.

I briefly thought of the thousands of soldiers, myriads of bands, millions of citizens, and hundreds of countries that have had this same feeling when the president arrives. Here I was, with the sound of river rolling over the rocks and salmon splashing and doing the death dance as they leaped up out of the water and hit on their stomachs to loosen their precious cargo of eggs. Osprey screeched overhead, and eagles circled around as if even they knew who was arriving. Alaskan nature would give our president the grandest welcome of all.

As he emerged from the plane, he stepped out onto the pontoon. Looking at me, he said, "Son, can I lean on you so I can get off this pontoon?"

"Yes sir, Mr. President," I replied. "You sure can, since we've been leaning on you for years."

He looked me over real good, and we both started laughing. We were off to a great start!

It was sobering to see how thorough and serious the Secret Service men became as they accompanied the president. They positioned their two boats on either side of mine. I was going to have an audience watching us fish whether I wanted one or not! All of them carried sufficient firepower. You may not believe this, but one of the Secret Service men was in a specially designed wet suit and kept up with us in another boat. When we drifted, he would jump in the water and float down the river with us. This suit must have been warm and well designed, because the river was ice-cold from the Alaskan snowmelt.

The president chose to fish with his grandson, Jeb Bush, from Florida. I was delighted! The son of the governor of Florida could really handle his fishing pole. Both of the Bushes were very experienced anglers.

The day was what I call "bluebird"—no clouds, no wind. The river sparkled like Perrier effervescent water. As we began our first float, I prayed for a quick hook-up. On the first cast, President Bush hooked an arctic char; in the same family as the brook trout or German brown, they are rollers and fighters. I saw the unbelief and then the sheer joy of both Jeb and the president as they caught fish after fish.

Suddenly I saw the president's pole double over. The line began screaming out. I knew immediately that he had snagged a log or rock "fish" —the pole wasn't bouncing, and because of our fast drift down the river, he was quickly running out of line and options.

I turned to quickly start the motor and heard a loud snap as the president's pole broke in half.

So . . . what do you say when the president breaks your pole? Absolutely nothing.

He handed me the useless pole and said, "I'm sorry, Rocky, but get me another one fast." That is exactly what I did. I had six poles prepared for the president so that if a line snapped or a pole broke, we could simply hand him a new one. We didn't waste any time, and neither did he.

While fishing, the president and I enjoyed pleasant conversation. I asked him some personal questions, because who in the world gets ten hours one day with the president right next to him? We also talked about the world and politics, but our great common interest was love for adventure. The president told me of avoiding sharks, skydiving, parachuting, and other exploits in his life. Then I told him what my wife had said: "He may be president, but he can never get pregnant!" She maintains that pregnancy is the greatest adventure of all.

We avoided deep and heady conversations but did touch briefly on what Noah may have done the entire time he was on the ark. Since Noah had a beautiful boat and lots of water, I suggested that he fished the whole time. Then the president reminded me that Noah only had two worms . . .

On occasion, the Secret Service frogman would float by the boat, and the president would catch a grayling or a char and hand it to the wet-suited man. The frogman would then ease over to a large gravel bar and toss the live, wiggling fish onto the sand. Two pairs of bald eagles would jockey with each other, talons extended, to enjoy this free lunch provided by the president. He told me he was very involved in legislation to preserve and protect the bald eagle, our nation's symbol, and he greatly enjoyed watching them in wild Alaska.

This was an absolutely perfect Alaskan day: incredible fishing, the president in my boat . . . I felt blessed.

As we continued drifting down the river, we caught at least six different species of fish. Northern pike, up to thirty pounds, are common in some Alaskan rivers, lakes, and sloughs. On our river we have pike weighing *over* thirty pounds and measuring over fifty inches long. Arctic char may weigh ten pounds or more and are not uncommon in our Alaskan rivers. As for grayling, the Holitna is absolutely chock-full of trophy grayling. We catch many equal to the current world record of twenty-three inches, four pounds thirteen ounces. Our chum salmon vary in size from four to over thirty pounds. Returning adult red salmon usually weigh between four and eight pounds; the largest we have caught was thirteen pounds. Of course, today we were fishing for the biggest prize of all, the Alaskan king salmon. The world record is ninety-seven pounds. We have caught kings (a.k.a. *chinook*) in the eighty-pound range on this very river.

When fishing, I always carry a fourteen-inch Rapala skinning knife. This knife is in a leather holster and is positioned so that I can pull it quickly to fillet fish, cut tangles, sever ropes, and perform a myriad of other necessary fishing guide tasks. The Secret Service had requested I not bring my .44 Magnum (bear discourager) but did not question this long, sharp knife conspicuously hanging on the front of my vest like a sword in its sheath.

I was busy changing lines and lures on the president's pole, and, without thinking, I unsheathed the shiny weapon right under the president's nose.

Suddenly, for one brief second, I was staring into the icy eyes of the Secret Service agents. "Don't shoot, don't shoot!" I pleaded under my breath, "Don't shoot! I'm only cutting his line!" I breathed a sigh of relief when the line was cut and their expressions lightened.

We kept slamming the fish, and on one drift the president had a record straight ten casts and ten fish boated.

As we drifted down this wild remote river, I suddenly saw something very unusual. There was another boat in the river, a rare sight. Sometimes we can go weeks without seeing another soul. Other adventurers on the river, especially guides, were seldom appreciated. Like finalists in a beauty pageant, guides may smile a lot, but there is *not* a lot of love shared.

As I drifted by the boat, I smiled and waved the "Alaskan wave." (you act like you're swatting mosquitoes with your right hand, making sure you look the other direction.)

As I swiped at the bugs and furtively glanced over at the other boat, I gave a slight start. I recognized both the boat and the guide. He was a very well-known, long-established guide in Alaska who had contributed the ultimate sacrifice in our line of work: he had lost a son in the bush.

As I floated across from the boat, I glanced at their empty fish box and the discouraged looks of the two big men fishing with this guide. They were fishless! I didn't want to gloat or feel superior (ha!), so I kept drifting. But just as we came even with them, the president hooked a huge king salmon, played it well, and we netted it about a half mile below the other guide and his clients. I'm sure they were watching and wondering when it would be their turn. I asked the president if he would like to do that again. His response? "Of course! Yes, yes! Let's do it!" I started the motor, went back upstream, and decided I would introduce the president and Jeb to this respected Alaskan guide.

As I approached their boat, anchored in a deep hole on the banks of the river, I throttled down and slowly eased my boat—and the president—toward the watching guide and fishermen.

Sprinkling his words with lots of profanity, the other guide yelled, "Get out of my fishing hole, Rocky! You don't own the river!"

I glanced at the president, feeling greatly embarrassed; I also glanced at the Secret Service entourage that were on both sides of us, expecting to hear the clicks of drawn weapons.

"Hey!" I stood up and shouted, calling the guide by name and hurriedly adding, "I just wanted you to meet the president! George Bush Sr.!"

An instant hush came over the river. The two huge Austrians in the other boat started speaking rapidly in German. They finally recognized who had just floated up. *"Mein Gott! Nein! Bush—Es ist Bush! Zieneifemmatterictderherr* . . . Well, I don't speak German, but you get the idea! Their cameras quickly preserved this moment of history.

Between the *click-click*s and the guttural oohs and aahs came this incredible reply from the guide (I will try to relay it word for word—minus the cussing): "Well, I'll be darned, Mr. Bush! You know, you need me! Yep, you should hire me to be your public relations manager all up and down this here river. Yep, I'll take $400,000 a year for that job—and I need that job too!"

Well, the president and I both just stared. Finally, I apologized for invading the other guide's fishing hole and muttered to the president, "Doggone Democrats. I'm truly sorry, sir. Truly sorry."

But he had a twinkle in his eye, and his only reply was, "Let's catch another one of those big kings!"

"Yes, sir!" I replied, and off we went.

We hooked a thirty-five-pound king salmon on the first drift. President Bush seemed intense and focused as he played the salmon. There was no smile, and he requested a quick net. I gladly complied. "Take me up to those other guys, Rocky," was his next strange request. I looked at him, wondering what was going on in that head, but did not question the Commander-in-Chief's order.

I dreaded pulling up to their boat, so I approached them slowly. The president and his big king were now on the very front of my vessel. Suddenly he shouted out, "Look at this one! Isn't he a dandy?" Then, "Isn't this a *great* fish?" All three men in the other boat gaped as the president gently lowered the giant king into the river and released his prize catch.

Mutterings were quickly drowned out as I eased the motor into reverse and, again, backed out of their fishing hole.

The president got such a kick out of this that we performed that same ritual twice more. I think he got his point across. I never enjoyed catch-and-release more than I did on this day. Later he wrote me the following:

July 10, 2003
flying Alaska + Mexe

GEORGE BUSH

Dear Rocky,
You sure gave Jeb and
me a great time on Tuesday.
OK, we lost some fish
because we didn't "yard arm"
them properly; but we caught
a lot and we did a lot better
than those 2 huge Austrians.

Rock I love your book.
Jeb is reading it as I write.
Here is a souvenir photo
signed by two Presidents, one
is your new, grateful friend,

Gy Bush

EIGHT

A Beauty to Lose

Alaska can be a cruel and beautiful mistress, exquisite one moment and a deceptive temptress the next. The life a guide chooses challenges to the marrow. This challenge is very personal and reaches to some of the deepest inroads of a person. Perhaps the most difficult aspect of living and working in Alaska is the temptation to indulge in singular introspection, constantly facing the wildness of nature, the running rivers and untamed wildlife that makes you come alive. I say it's a temptation because it's both a beautiful thing and a dangerous thing. The geographical distance and days or months away from family enhances the relational distance too. Alaska itself offers something desirous to be sought, but it can come at a price if you indulge too much. The distance, the wildness, the challenge can push the threshold in your heart and mind and, when you're a guide, in your relationships. And yet my guide skills encourage the journey that most often compels my guests to come to Alaska.

My family and I love to host those looking for the challenge. I have always obsessed with giving every guest at my lodge the dream trip of his or her life. My family and I have often joined together to fulfill the expectations of every Alaskan adventure. My wife, Sharon, the glue that holds the lodge together, handles the scheduling, staff, complaints, and all the little details I would never have time for. But even more than her practical role, Sharon adds an irreproducible charm to the Alaskan wilderness. I am enchanted with her beauty. She is a strikingly lovely, long-legged, California golden blonde with a wonderful, genuine personality and a gifted mind. She is loved by staff and guests alike and always has time for everyone. I am truly privileged to be her husband, and her presence in the Alaskan wild is a constant reminder of warmth and connection. My four darling daughters are blessings, too, and by their teenage years could fish better than nearly all the guests. At the lodge, they helped with meals, cleaning, entertainment, and numerous other chores.

Me? I went out on guided flying and boating trips with my guests. I packed, cleaned, and processed game, then stumbled in late at night totally exhausted. It doesn't get dark in the summer in Alaska until 3:00 or 4:00 a.m., so it is easy to forget how late it is. I learned the hard way not to tell my daughters, "Come in when it gets dark!" Oh, they *loved* that!

"Sure, Dad!" they would say with big grins on their faces.

Our type of operation in remote Alaska involves lots of planning, fishing gear, food, shore lunches, guide training, regulations, boats, permits, planes, pilots, and, well, you get the picture. What isn't seen is the stress a job like this puts on a marriage, even a good one. Having four girls has its own stresses, especially with young teenagers. But this career has added challenges. I doubt any studies have been done on marriages of professional guides. I suspect, though, that the divorce rate is very high. My wife and I were often separated for months by several thousand miles during hunting and fishing season. Plus, after I got home, I would often travel extensively to book clients for the next year. Owning a business has its own extra set of pressures. When financial issues arise and bills come due, it is especially difficult since there are no guaranteed or regular paychecks.

The practical demands of owning a business, the guide's life of separation, and the lure of the Alaskan wilderness frame these next experiences that have shaken the core of my life, belief, and love for my family and wife.

During one of our seasons, Elmer and Gloria, Sharon's parents, were staying at our house in California while we were away. They loved to barbecue, and Gloria had put some salmon on the grill located on a second-level enclosed porch thirty feet from a cement patio below. It was a very hot day in the Sacramento area, and the temperature reached a sizzling 107 degrees. I had left two full propane tanks for the barbecue, but unknown to us one had been fatefully overfilled. The warmth from the barbecue and the sun heated up the small enclosed porch, and the safety gas valve broke on the overfilled tank with a loud *pop*. Alarmed, Gloria said to Elmer, "Did you hear that?"

Elmer replied, "No, what?"

"I heard a loud pop from the barbecue!" Gloria answered, and she got up to investigate.

As she neared the sliding door, Elmer yelled, "Hey, you're not going out there!"

She stopped, startled, and explained, "But it's Sharon's house, and it could catch on fire or something. I need to check."

Elmer, always the gentleman, replied firmly, "You're not going out there, honey; I'll go turn it off."

Propane vapor had been leaking from the broken safety valve and was building up in a dangerous mist under and around the still-burning barbecue. As Elmer approached, he mumbled something about this "white mist." He was wearing sandals, shorts, and no shirt.

As he bent over in front of the barbecue and began fiddling with the controls, the whole area suddenly exploded. Doors blew off, windows blew out, and debris went everywhere. Fire rolled like a red ball into the house, singeing cabinets, burning the floor, and searing Gloria's legs and feet. Elmer was thrown up like a rag doll into the air and landed on his back on the cement pad almost thirty feet below.

Elmer was seventy-eight, barrel-chested, and big and tough, but this was a horrendous explosion. He had received the full force directly against his shirtless body, been burned extensively, and thrown sky-high. He landed on concrete with nothing to break his fall, smashing his back and head. Gloria rushed to his side. Why wasn't he out cold—or dead? Who could survive that? Yet, here he was, shaken, but calmly telling Gloria, "I think I need to go to the hospital."

She drove him to Roseville Hospital, and from there he was immediately transferred to the UC Davis Health System's Burn Center in Sacramento. Gloria prayed through the night that her gentle Christian giant would survive. The next day she called Sharon in Alaska.

We were clipping along in one of our busiest seasons—lots of clients, lots of fish, lots of fun . . . and lots of work. Right smack in the middle of a very busy week, Gloria called. Sharon picked up the phone and I could recognize Gloria's voice on the other end. Sharon's facial expressions were not good.

"Mom, should I come home?" Sharon asked.

"No," Gloria responded. "I don't think it will be that bad. I think he will be OK. Just hold on for a day, and we'll see what happens."

Sharon hung up the phone with a feeling of urgency. She was very concerned about her dad who had always been the indestructible force in his family, larger than life and in good health. The next day, however, their pastor called and talked to Sharon. "Sharon," he began, "as your parents' pastor, I am deeply concerned. I really think you need to come home."

"This is really serious, isn't it?" she asked.

He answered solemnly, "Yes, it's really serious."

Gloria was also reeling under the situation. Her legs and feet were burned, her husband was badly hurt, and now her heart began beating irregularly. She, too, was admitted to the hospital.

Sharon threw a few things together and left that evening. She hated to go but knew she had to. She flew all night and part of the next day—to Anchorage, Seattle, and eventually to Sacramento. It was a brutal trip, and she was in transit over thirty hours. Her good friend Cathy picked her up at the airport, and they drove straight to UC Davis.

Sharon was ushered in to see her dad, and he was heavily bandaged but was sitting up and trying to eat something. Initially this reassured Sharon and gave her hope. She kissed him and said, "I love you, Daddy."

"I love you too," he whispered through his bandages. Then they had a brief but memorable father-daughter chat. Later, Sharon and I would both believe that it was God who had made it possible for Sharon to travel thousands of miles without ticket reservations and still arrive in time to share these last special few moments with her dad.

Within hours he was put on a ventilator and, due to his pain, had to be drugged heavily. He could respond physically a little and seemed to understand things said to him, but he was not able to communicate verbally.

Sharon went to visit and console her mom who was upstairs in the same hospital. Thankfully, her mom was doing better. Sharon told her how encouraging it had been to see her dad sitting up and talking. Shortly after this, Sharon collapsed from exhaustion and finally got some much-needed sleep.

A few hours later, she called me and told me about Elmer's condition and described their conversation. I was happy to hear that Elmer was alive, but I was sobered by his condition.

Meanwhile, what was going on at the lodge was sobering too.

We hired an assistant for Sharon just before she left, and this lady had been pushed into a major role immediately. She was having a difficult time handling the girls and working in an unfamiliar position. Another guide and his wife had also assumed more responsibilities, and they, too, were finding out how hard Sharon's shoes were to fill. I felt overwhelmed. My staff was grumpy and ready to revolt. Somehow my personal family cabin became staff headquarters. I deeply resented this further intrusion. My only sanctuary had been invaded. I was ready to blow up. There was also a big group there that week that had arrived expecting the "trip of a lifetime," and they deserved the best I could give them.

I was normally a funny guy. I made people laugh. My fun spirit, though, had flatlined. I had no laughter in my heart. I was hollow.

I had always prided myself on providing magical weeks for my guests. My reputation, my family, and my business depended on it. Now I was straining to find a solution.

My four girls struggled to cope. They were worried about their granddaddy. But they tried hard to help me and the staff. I knew it was difficult for them without their mom there to hold them, scold them, and love them. Even I was barely afloat since Sharon had left. She was the light of my lodge—the light of my *life!*—and our shining lamp was gone. I knew I needed a diversion to keep me sane.

Caribou season was only days away, and I tried to focus on that, but my mind kept wandering to California. To better focus, I flew some scouting missions and discovered where a huge herd of caribou were gathering in preparation for their fall migration. It was one of the most amazing sites I had ever seen, thousands upon thousands of caribou. From our bird's-eye view, the mountains looked like they were alive with the movement of all the caribou. the Alaskan Mulchatna herd was estimated to have two hundred thousand caribou.

I excitedly told my guests what I had seen. "There's a catch, though," I told them. "Hunting season isn't open yet, so it's sightseeing only, and the caribou are in an almost impossible location to get to, but what a sight it would be to see!" I thought ruefully, *Ain't that the way it always is? The best just out of reach!*

One of the guests that week was more than a client or a casual friend. Eric Eilertsen and I had shared some wilderness excursions together that caused a lifelong bond. That bond gave him the courage to approach me.

"Rock," he said, "just how tough would it be to get to those caribou?" Eric knew I would be totally honest with him.

I pursed my lips and said, "There is a winding, rocky river that leads up to it, but only the devil himself would run it. It is one of the most beautiful spots in the region, but I don't think anyone has ever been able to navigate that river, and with a regular boat it is impossible." I paused meaningfully but saw the gleam in Eric's eye.

"Well, Rock," he said, almost prophetically, "the devil ain't got nothin' on you! My friend Bryan and I have discussed it, and we can't stand it! We want to take a crack at that river and are dying to see those caribou!"

I replied slowly, "Well . . . I do have that souped-up jet boat—" knowing that a risky river run would help divert my attention from California. I wasn't sure if that's what I should do, but I pushed on, telling myself it was for the sake of my guests.

"See?" he interrupted my trailing thoughts. "You are such an unconventional guy; I knew you had a way!"

"There are no guarantees," I cautioned him. "It'll be very dangerous, and someone could get hurt."

Eric replied, "Well, I didn't come all the way up here to ride ferry boats!"

Now I was starting to get a chill. Could I run this river? I was good at running rivers. Top guides are judged on this ability. I had honed this craft over years of experience and crashes. Every true winner has had his share of crashes.

I reflected on one such crash when I had been running the Tazimna River and had hit a log and gotten flipped out of the boat. As the boat swung around backward, I somehow managed to grab the gunwales and was pulled downriver, trailing the boat in the water like a streamer. Finally, I was able to climb back in and continue my journey, pride askew but teeth intact. Because of experiences like this, I could read a river like the morning paper—most of the time. Reading a river is also like reading a woman, though. She gives out hints about what is in her depths, but if you aren't careful, it is easy to get her wrong! Rivers and women—both enigmas, wrapped in riddles.

Wind, rain, boat speed, fog, water clarity, and available light affect the ability to read a river's clues, and they must be read at a moment's notice. Submerged rocks and brush; hidden sandbars and stumps; and the scourge of all rivers, the "widow maker," create unique eddies, currents, and ripples that give only faint clues as to their origin and identification. Appropriately named, a "widow maker" is a tree that has broken or fallen into the river, and the branches and top have usually worn off. The heavier trunk portion is partially anchored on the bottom; the rest of the tree is facing downriver, bobbing just beneath the surface. It often moves, bumping slowly downriver and winding up in places that had previously been clear sailing.

Running into a widow maker while traveling downstream is like running up a ramp. It will launch and flip your boat high into the air at all kind of angles and will flip and separate you from your senses. ('Course, I've been separated from mine for a while.) Conversely, going upstream and hitting a widowmaker is like hitting a brick wall. Yes, running a river is a difficult skill, but it is also addictive, like many challenges. And I could run rivers and get to places others couldn't get to. This afforded my more daring guests a chance to see, fish, and hunt in pristine areas that were almost untouched. I hoped *we* would make it untouched.

My jet boat was built to run in very shallow water. The 90-horsepower outboard on it had no props; instead, the lower unit dipped into the water only about three inches below the stern. Powerful streams of air are forced though this unit, propelling the boat. The back of almost any boat is lower in the water at low speeds. To get on "step" or "plane" so the boat is up more on top of the water and running level, power and speed are required. To run on step in my jet boat, I needed to get up to at least fifteen or twenty miles per hour and could easily run over thirty. The great thing about being on step is that the boat could run in very shallow water. The bad news was that running in shallow water at high speed was when it was most dangerous! And that's not all.

Normally boats have a keel or rudder or a V-shaped hull that carves the water, affording bite and providing stability and maneuverability. This was a light aluminum, flat-bottom boat. There was nothing on the bottom to dig in the water and create resistance for turning. Turning was accomplished by skidding sideways on top of the water. Steering was reminiscent of navigating a sharp turn at high speeds in a '57 Chevy with bald tires on a loose gravel road. Oh yeah, this would be fun!

I had fully discussed the dangers of this challenging adventure with my longtime friends, but the lure of seeing the huge herd of caribou was something they were willing to go to almost any lengths to do. Our main fear was simply not being able to "run the river" far enough or high enough to get to them. Bottoming out or crashing into the riverbank was bothersome and could cause potential harm but seemed an acceptable risk to all of us for what was at stake.

From our lodge it was about ten miles across the lake to Chulitna Bay. The Chulitna River empties there, and this winding, cold river cascades another fifteen or so miles down from Long Lake, often forming rapids in the process. A short climb from Long Lake up the mountain would get us to the caribou. We would need to leave early in the morning. I packed a number of five-gallon cans of gas; an orange emergency gear pack with a first-aid kit, dry clothes, survival gear, and a firearm; and, of course, some Swisher Sweets and hot coffee! Eric wrote later of this trip, "Bryan and I were like kids at Christmas. Grown men giddy with the prospect of going to a place where few had gone before, up a river that could not be navigated, to see a sight more amazing than any other I have ever seen in my life."

We set off across a calm lake, giving me a chance to practice my turning skills with my jet toy. During one long turn my thoughts and prayers spontaneously drifted to Elmer and my family. It had always been him and me against our combined six girls. He was my comrade and bulwark in *those* deep waters!

I've got to hand it to Bryan and Eric. Both were a bit out of their elements. Bryan is a computer wizard, and Eric is a very successful entrepreneur, yet here they were, gleefully facing a life-threatening adventure. I smiled at the eagerness on their faces and the excitement in their voices. We reached the mouth of the river without incident and looked for an opening up this treacherous river. It resembles a snake as it winds up the mountain. And like a snake, it can lie in ambush and strike out of nowhere. The mouth of the river is inviting, though, and gives a false sense of security that belies the dangers to come. I approached confidently, picked a channel, and shot through.

We were seemingly crawling along at about five miles an hour but in reality were going twenty or more miles an hour, because the swiftness of the current against us often exceeded fifteen. I was able to gain extra speed in some of the calmer areas as we slowly progressed upriver. We hadn't gone far when I lost traction in a turn and skidded sideways into the bank. Everyone saw it coming and braced.

Oh no! I lost my cigar! Sharon would've loved that!

This "skid turning" was tricky on calm water and really a puzzle on this curling river. Because the water was very shallow in places where we bottomed out or crashed into the bank, we had to drift back to deeper water so I could gain speed, get on top of the water (also known as "getting on step"), and be able to stay afloat and navigate these shallow hairpin turns. This occurred four or five times, but Eric and Bryan were actually getting a kick out of it and realized why this river was not meant to be navigated by boat. No harm was done, and amazingly we kept making progress.

About halfway we stopped for lunch at the confluence of another river. It was a particularly beautiful spot, and Eric couldn't help but try out a new Mepps lure. He caught several beautiful grayling.

Suddenly he noticed on the sandbar next to his foot a huge bear track over an inch deep in the hard gravel! Eric is well over two hundred pounds, and his own footprints weren't even visible, so that was some heavy bear! The footprint was much wider than the span of a man's hand and very long. I estimated the bear at close to a thousand pounds and up to ten feet tall.

Eric's observation said it all: "It is clear that we are strangers trespassing in this giant bear's backyard. You may believe you are important back in the city, town, or office that you came from, but here you are just a snack!"

We continued upriver, and the mountains began to close in around us. The scenery was simply spectacular. The further we got upriver, the tougher it was to navigate. The trick was to stay in the deepest available parts of the water. The river would separate into two or three wide, shallow channels, and I had to make instant decisions. Some of these channels were probably no more than four or five inches deep. I was standing in the middle of the boat behind the steering wheel, intently focused on reading the water, current, ripples, and eddies just ahead.

I fell into a zone.

I was outside of myself, watching, almost clairvoyantly anticipating the river's every obstacle. A rock here, a log there, I swerved slightly and bounced a ripple to get less than an inch of lift. Everything was precise and fast. I felt like I couldn't do anything wrong and I could see all the river's traps. The tension was building as the entrance to the lake approached. I strained to keep my focus, my guests hugging the sides of the boat, trying to keep it equally weighted. Then, like a long exhale, we broke free and onto Long Lake!

I had done it! I had made it all the way! We were all stoked. But my celebration was muted because I knew that I could not share this moment with Sharon now or when I returned to the lodge. I also knew the upcoming run downriver would be tougher and more hazardous!

I once said to a friend about running rivers, "You know, I can run a river a hundred times perfectly and maybe *one* time hit a rock or a stump, and that's all that gets talked about and remembered."

He laughed and said, "Son, it is the same in many professions. A preacher, for instance, can live honorably for years, deliver great sermons, and avoid all of Satan's traps. But let him mess up just once and that will become his label, and can—and will—ruin his life as a pastor. Remember, it just takes one small ink stain to ruin a beautiful gown."

Now I have a saying to help keep me in step: "Miss all the logs!"

We got out of our boat, and climbed up the side of the mountain. What awaited us at the top was almost spiritual. Eric described it well when he wrote me later:

Even in my mind's eye I could never imagine a sight as beautiful as what awaited us on the top of the mountain. In front of us was an elevated valley filled with thousands of caribou gathering before they began their migration. The clouds hung just above us as though they were protecting this magnificent sight. In a tree off to our right just 50 yards away was an eagle's nest and the mother called to us perhaps a little anxious as she stood on the edge of her nest. We could see a grizzly bear along the edge of the valley. This is the most magnificent sight I have ever seen, God's incredible creation filled with his creatures as I could never imagine or have ever seen since. This must have been what the Garden of Eden looked like. If not, it was close. The river, the mountains, the majestic trees, the animals, and the weather were all on display in pristine perfection. All around us was untouched nature in perfect balance.

No one spoke for quite a while as we absorbed this sight. In unison, as if moved by a gentle force, we were compelled to silently worship in recognition of God's awesome power and creation. We felt a deep bond among ourselves and with nature. It was a moment I wanted to share with the one I love.

We had conquered much to get here. We simply sat, stared, and shared and let it seep through and saturate us. It was a time of rejuvenation of our spirits and a special connection with nature. We must have lingered there, soaking it all in, for a couple of hours, each deep in his own thoughts and enthralled and inspired by the sheer impact this scene had on us. I honestly think we were looking at about forty thousand caribou or more!

The floating clouds began to block the sun, and we regrettably had to go. We got into the boat, and I told Bryan and Eric to make sure their life vests were cinched up tight.

Bryan reacted with concern. "What's wrong?"

"It's harder to get on step going downriver, so our speed will be a lot greater," I said. "If the current is fifteen miles per hour, we need an extra fifteen miles or more to get on step. Our true speed will be thirty miles an hour or more! It is too shallow up here to drift much, so we'll have to run hard to get on plane. Coming upriver, it is easier because the water runs directly into the hull of the boat, pushing the boat higher." Then I thought to myself, *Yeah, just one more reason this hasn't been tried before!* I didn't tell them the lack of sunlight would make it even harder to read the river ahead.

I hated to start the motor and break the serene stillness of this place, so we drifted a few moments so I could psych myself up for the trip downriver. Then the motor roared to life and we were off!

The darkening clouds obscuring the sun combined with a chilly wind. Decreased light made the water dark and hard to see into, and the wind and rain rippled the surface of the river, making it almost impossible to interpret those special eddies and swirls warning of trouble. Going downstream, the boat was harder to steer. Eric was in the back, head down under his hood to escape the rain and clutching the sides of the boat tightly. Bryan was tucked head down in the front, trying to stay out of the cold wind. After the boat slipped and slid dangerously around a few turns, it got really quiet. Everyone sensed we were in grave peril.

I was in deep concentration and chewing on my wet cigar vigorously. I disdained the protection of the windshield, instead standing erect and peering over it to see the water better. The cold rain and wind pelted my face. I strained to keep the boat in the deepest parts of the channels. I saw a smooth section of water ahead, increased velocity, and navigated our speeding craft toward this seemingly safe passage. Too late I realized my mistake.

A large, flat-topped rock just beneath the surface was the cause of the smooth water. We were going close to thirty miles an hour. All I had time to do was yell, "LOOK OUT!"

The boat slammed into the rock and went airborne, twisting sideways. My face smashed into the windshield, ripping apart my chin. I don't ever recall being hit harder in my life. I was tossed into the air as if from a trampoline. I felt myself spinning in space and doing a complete flip. Then I waited for the darkness that I expected to follow when I came down.

I crashed into the water with terrific force and submerged, dragging along the bottom. Somehow I landed without hitting anything solid or being struck again by the boat. I struggled to the surface and could not understand why water was filling up my lungs even though my mouth was tightly closed. I soon discovered that my lower chin was split wide open, allowing water to flow freely into my mouth. I was spitting water and blood, but I was conscious. I was stunned and terrified for my companions. Where were Bryan and Eric?

Here is how Eric later described what happened to him:

The next few minutes were like something out of a movie. The world went into slow motion. There is a sense that you are watching yourself on a movie screen. My first sensation is that I'm flying through the air helpless with no ability to control my path. I have a sense of being upside down but still in the air. Then there is a crash so severe I feel like I have been tackled by the whole National Football League at the same time.

The next sensation is that I am under water holding my breath in a very tight space. I am moving through the water at a fast pace but I can not move. My body can feel the blows as I crash into the river bottom. There is something pressing down on me and all I can see is murky water. The boat was on top of me, keeping me pinned against the bottom of the river. My twisted life-vest was keeping me from being able to move. I was for the first time in my life truly helpless. This wild ride continued for some time. No matter how much I struggled, I could not get out from under the boat. The current was too swift and there was just no room between the river bottom and the boat.

After some time I remember relaxing. I had come to the end of holding my breath. This was it. It was a strange peace without panic. I had done my best and was willing to accept whatever was coming next.

Suddenly, without explanation and with no recollection of how, I popped out on the surface of the water. I remember drawing a deep breath and choking but I was alive and lying on my back in the water. I floated to a gravel bar where I stood up. The boat was upside down with a huge dent in the bow. There was blood on the boat. I could see Rocky hanging on to the boat with one hand and holding on to Bryan's collar with his other.

When Bryan was thrown from the boat, the bow slammed into his knee. He flipped end over end, crashing hard into the water. He was numb and dazed and struggling to keep his balance in the current. He held on to a rock until I was able to get to him. His kneecap was dislocated, and ligaments were torn. Bryan was in a great deal of pain and was moaning. I was dazed, too, but could sense that Bryan was going into shock, and the cold river was draining him of his strength. He was too weak to move on his own, so I dragged him to shore. He sat on the bank, shivering in the chilly air and wet clothes. The boat had sunk to the bottom, turning sideways, partially filling with water, but it was only three or four feet deep, so it was not completely submerged. Most of the gear and contents had been dumped into the river and had sunk or was floating downstream. To survive we needed to find a way to retrieve some of our gear.

I looked and saw our only gas tank and the emergency survival pack floating away. Eric saw the same and beat feet along the shore, almost five hundred yards, to intercept. Those were critical items, and it was imperative that they were recovered. When he returned, exhausted, I babbled at him with my busted lip, "Good job Eric. Now let's build a fire so we can dry out." I knew Bryan was in trouble and needed to get as warm and dry as possible. One of the gas cans was still tied to the boat, and we poured some of its gas on a downed tree on the gravel bar. Matches from the emergency bag allowed us to start a nice fire.

Fortunately the rain had stopped, and we stripped off our wet clothes, wrung them out, and let the hot fire start drying them.

With evening approaching we sat there almost naked in forty-degree weather in remote Alaska, knowing outside help was far away and unavailable, maybe for days. There was no way another boat could run this river. It was accessible only by helicopter, and no one even knew exactly where we were. My chin now sported a huge gash, and it was cut clean through to the bone. I was having a lot of difficulty talking. The pain kept me focused and sharp.

We were in a canyon area, would be very difficult to spot, and our radio, recovered from the emergency bag, was not getting good reception. After repeated attempts I was only able to relay to the staff at the lodge that we had had a bad accident. They knew our intended route and alerted search and rescue. Search and rescue, however, would not even begin their search until the next day. Not even they fly in the bush at night in Alaska. On the rare occasion a bush pilot is unable to avoid a night flight and gets trapped in the dark, it is referred to as "dog bark" flying: the pilot flies low with his windows open, guessing at where villages may be and listening for barking dogs. (Dogs are a pilot's best friends too.) Then they circle and try to locate a possible makeshift airstrip or homemade clearing.

Meanwhile, Sharon, my best friend, was in a desperate situation. Elmer's condition was getting grave. His heart was failing, his lungs were filling with fluid, and his kidneys were struggling. Elmer was in great pain and unable to communicate. He had repeatedly told his family that if he were ever in a situation where he was beyond restoration to a decent quality of life, he did not want to be kept alive. Sharon, her mother, and the rest of her family were now struggling with this issue. Elmer had always seemed so strong that it was hard to believe he could not recover. Even the hospital staff initially felt he would survive. Sharon and Gloria wanted to give Elmer more time to see if there was any possibility of this, but some in her family wanted to end his pain and abide by his strongly stated wishes. It was a tough decision for the family to make. Removing her daddy's life support system was more than Sharon could bear. She desperately wanted my input and to let me know her dad was dying.

Cell phones were not allowed in the hospital, so she asked her friend Cathy to call my lodge. The lodge took Cathy's call right after I had reported to them our boat crash. When Cathy returned to the hospital, she told Sharon, "Rocky has been in a terrible accident. No one knows where he is or what happened." Needless to say, Sharon was horrified. She could lose her husband and her father in the same day!

Her husband was trying desperately not to be a statistic! My chin was a mess, and I was bleeding, but the fire had warmed us, and our clothes were now dry enough to wear. I knew that we needed to get back to the lodge as soon as possible to tend to the wounds caused by the crash. Our only real choice was to find a way to use our boat. Eric was fast at work on that. He located a water pump submerged in the boat and attached it to the terminals of the still-strapped-in boat battery. The pump began working and slowly emptying the water from the boat. We then used paddles and sticks to try and leverage the boat right side up. Eric began splashing out some of the water with the paddle. We checked the gas hose connector, and amazingly it did not appear damaged. The gas hose was still connected to the gas tank Eric had recovered, and it fit snugly on the motor. The motor had been submerged during the crash, so I had little hopes it would start. Our only battery was being used to run the water pump, and I was concerned that it would get too weak to start the boat motor. I did not want to remain and become a snack for that giant grizzly whose footprint we had seen!

That little water pump was amazing. It finally pumped the last of the water out of the boat. We blew the water out of the carburetor and hose as best we could with our mouths, hooked everything back up, and turned the key. *Varooom!* That baby started on the first try! Purred like a kitten! And I gotta tell you, that was one sweet sound to our ears!

Now it was time for the really hard part: getting back in the boat that had nearly killed us. It was like that old saying about crawling back into the saddle of the very horse that had bucked you. I also knew we did not have enough gas to get all the way back. Our fear was palpable, but we knew we had no choice. We crawled in reluctantly, gritted our teeth, and set off down the treacherous river.

It began raining again, and the wind was ice-cold against my face. This turned out to be a blessing, because the near-freezing water pelting my chin was like covering it with ice. It numbed up and stopped bleeding. We raced down the river, and I kept fighting for control of the boat. I prayed silently for guidance as I tried to navigate past and around more of the river's deadly hidden obstacles. I was numb, tired, frozen, and apprehensive, yet I felt more intensely alive than I can possibly describe. The wilderness, my home, is both my security and my greatest danger. To be coughed up one more time from the jaws of death electrified me with respect and awe and of course got my adrenaline pumping.

We raced on in the dim light, Bryan huddled in the front and Eric curled up in the back. As the "death boat" sped toward home, I searched along the river for any extra gas cans that had floated

The Alaskan Range keeps Western Alaska wild

Coming home by air, the only way to get home

Big toys for adventuresome boys

A beautiful place to scout and
to soak in pristine nature

Our snowy egress to the log cabin

Midnight in June in Remote Alaska

At the end of the day, it's a great feeling
to put your arm around a (harmless) friend.

Sheefish, Greyling, Charr, Salmon, Pike . . .
what is on the end of my line?

Exercising our "Playboy" rule: Catch and Release

This picture tells the incredible story of a great hunt!
PS The moose ribs are a delicacy.

I think this moose was a Baptist after He answered our call.

This caribou scored high in Boone and Crockett
and Safari Club because of his mass and symmetry.

A Son stands tall after a caribou hunt with Dad . . .
what a great Alaskan Adventure.

The Interior Alaskan Grizzly is one of the main culprits
in our disappearing Alaskan Moose population.

Well, Mr. President...let me fix that fishing line!

Drifting into the Alaskan
World of Adventure

My hat is off to you, Mr. President!

The Call of the Wild . . . can you hear it?

A Wild River is like a woman,
it's trying to tell you something but you have to listen!

Someone was there
just before us

A welcome sight from a hunter's tent

Part of the Mulchatna Caribou Herd in Western Alaska

The famous Alaska "Red" Salmon
and the just-as-famous pitcher, David Dravecky

A Happy Hunter
with an absolute trophy
caribou (notice that the
horns are in velvet)

Two great encouragers
to me: Chuck Swindoll
and my Bro, Dave.

All you see of caribou on the run.

"OK" I say to Jared, my pilot,
"Find a place to land us on this mountain ridge."

Gruesome, I know, but this is the danger of Alaska
up close and personal.

The guardians of the wildest place on the planet

ANCHORAGE, AK 238 m

SLEETMUTE, AK 16 m

PORT
ALSWORTH, AK 120 m

AUBURN, CA 2,177 m

SISTERS, OR 1,821 m

SANDPOINT, ID 1,989 m

ROCKLIN, CA 2,178 m

Our tribute to "M.A.S.H." reminds us of how far we are from anywhere!

downriver. The first ones we located were empty, but we were in luck—we found one that wasn't. We poured what was left into our gas tank. How far would it take us? There was only one way to find out! Onward we flew.

At last we reached the final bend leading to the lake. What a difference, though! The lake that had been calm was now frothing with four- to five-foot waves and whitecaps. I called the lodge on the radio. They were relieved to hear from us, but because of the rough water, no one was confident enough to challenge the lake. We would have to make a run for it. We had little gas and ten tough miles to go. If we stalled in the middle of this heaving lake, we would be at the mercy of the waves with no way to keep the bow into the wind. We would likely be swamped and drown. So I told the lodge to set out on a specific compass heading and start searching for us if we weren't back in one hour. Our fate would be determined in the next sixty minutes!

I set out across the lake, bouncing on the waves and crabbing the boat into the wind. I prayed that God would keep refilling the gas tank as He had refilled the jars of oil for the poor widow. The motor kept humming, and I kept praying: "Oil, God, oil—I mean, gas, God, gas!"

Thirty minutes passed, and the motor still purred along. I strained my eyes for Hardenburg Cove, where our lodge is located. Finally, through the rain, darkness, and high waves, we saw a light. We were going to make it . . . alive! We sailed into the bay and beached at the lodge. Much later, when Eric checked our tank, he told me, "Rock, there wasn't enough gas left to fill a coffee cup!"

The welcoming crew included eight doctors who were guests that week. They helped us out of the boat, took care of Bryan right away, and hustled me into the lodge to tend to my chin.

They laid me on an Amana freezer top. I looked up at the circle of faces hovering over me and could hear them whispering. "Don't have any Novocain." "It'll hurt too much." "That is deep."

The slash in my chin had created a big hole right under my mouth. It looked as if I had *two* mouths, one on top of the other. When I tried to talk, the lower "mouth" would flap and gurgle. I'm sure I resembled a character out of a comic book. "OK," I burbled, "give it to me straight. What is going on?" The doctors couldn't help but laugh at my double mouth flapping up and down.

The pediatrician took the lead. "Well, Rock, you need to be stitched up, but none of us has any local anesthetic. It'll hurt like blazes, and you won't be able to stay still enough."

I had a suture needle in a first-aid kit and some fishing line. I gritted my teeth and tried to sound tough. "Just stitch me up! I can take it!"

I heard more chuckling, then, "All right, Rock. We have a gynecologist, a foot doctor, a general practitioner, a veterinarian, and several others. Which one do you want?"

"The gynecologist!" I gushed. That brought the house down! But for once I wasn't trying to be funny. I just figured the gynecologist would be the gentlest. Man, what a mistake! It was *painful*! He stuck that needle in my mouth, through my chin, and back out, over and over—and grinned the whole time! I nearly passed out.

I received twelve stitches without anesthesia. My oldest daughter, Ginger, was standing next to me, holding my hand and trying to offer comfort. She is exceptionally strong and more than holds her own with the men in guiding, packing meat, and fishing. Each time the needle would pierce me, she would give my hand a little squeeze. What she didn't realize was that every time the needle was inserted, it impacted her too. I could hear her suck in air quickly and then let out an audible gasp. Soon her gentle squeezes turned into full-blooded vise grips. I don't know which hurt worse, my lip being punctured or my hand being crushed.

I was too proud to back out, so I stiffened up, kept my teeth tightly clinched, and never moved. Today, I still sport a ragged scar on my chin.

Next time I'll choose the veterinarian.

I stumbled to my cabin and don't even remember removing my boots or crawling into bed. My chin was beginning to throb and swell, making my mouth look really big—like a puffer fish. The pain would have kept me awake if I had not been so exhausted. The letdown after an intense episode like I experienced can almost debilitate you. Every nerve, muscle, and fiber of my being had been pushed to the limit for hours. I physically and emotionally crashed into a profound sleep.

Suddenly I felt myself being rocked, water closing in over my face. I struggled to breathe, and someone was calling for help!

"Rock! Rock! Get up!"

"Wha—? Whut is it? Whu um I?"

"Rock, get up! You're in your cabin! They're waiting for you!"

Relief flooded me as realization set in. It was time to go fishing. My guests were waiting. Ouch! It hurt to move my mouth. Ouch! It hurt to breathe. My whole body ached. Ouch! *Ouch!* Get in a boat? Not a happy thought. I stumbled out of bed fully dressed and was greeted with some sweet humor.

"Daddy, Daddy, you look funny! Why do you have fishing line stuck on your chin?" inquired Merilee, daughter number two. I wanted to quip, "Well, I was swimming along and saw this tasty-looking worm on a hook . . ."

"Your face is all red and puffy," said Kelly, daughter number three.

"I want my mommy," chimed in Sunny, daughter number four.

"Lubb you guys too," I managed to barely grunt, then, "Hud from ya mum?"

They looked at me, trying to figure out what I had said, without laughing. "No, Dad," one finally replied, "and we are worried." She then gave me a big hug. Ouch again! It was worth it, though.

When I got to the dock, I saw a group waiting. "Hey, Rock! The fish are waiting!" one of my guests called out.

I should call Sharon, I thought. I checked the time, but it was early, and Sharon would probably still be asleep. I would call her as soon as I got back.

"This is going to be a long day, son," I told myself.

It *was* a long day. First time I've ever been quiet in a boat. The guests told me they had a really great time, and I wondered if my being quiet had anything to do with it . . . Nah!

Man, did my face hurt. My heart was hurting too. I said a silent prayer for Elmer as we boated back to the plane and took off for the lodge. During the flight back I was again very quiet.

When we landed on the lake and began to taxi toward the lodge, my heart sank. I could see my four girls standing on the beach, huddled together and crying. I knew immediately that Elmer had died. Their grandpa, my comrade, was gone.

I jumped out onto the pontoon of the plane, and as soon as the plane got close enough, jumped into the water and rushed to my girls. We hugged and wept. Elmer had always been a big part of their lives, and now he would never hold them again.

My face was numb, my heart was numb, and my mind was numb. I was straining to understand it all when I received Sharon's call. I knew she was grieving, but for some reason it was difficult to emotionally connect with her. It didn't make sense to me. I was struggling with her tragedy, but I couldn't make it mine. I tried to console her, but the words sounded shallow.

"The girls need to come down for the funeral," she was saying.

Huh? This hadn't occurred to me. Take the four girls away? For the rest of the year? Of course they had to go, but what was I going to do? They were a huge part of the staff. We were barely afloat without Sharon, and now they had to go?

"Uh, okay," I mumbled. "So sorry about Elmer . . ." I trailed off. More of the same disconnect, and the call ended.

What was going on? Why wasn't I there for her? I knew she was devastated by the loss of her dad and needed me, but I had not met that need. We were both trying to survive in two separate worlds, and both were falling apart.

Ginger took her three sisters and flew out of the Alaskan bush. When the girls left, the laughter and soul of the lodge left with them. The staff was overloaded and about to mutiny. How we made it through the next two weeks, I'll never know. I did know that my blonde beauty was far away and hurting. But since that call, I was avoiding even talking to her. I felt inadequate and did not want to face that fact head-on. I could stand up to a charging grizzly but could not face this. Why had I shut down on her when she needed me? Did I feel abandoned because all my girls had left? Did I resent that my career choice prevented me from being with them? I would be there if I had chosen a different path. Had I placed my job, our means of survival, ahead of my family? Do other men have these concerns? Do they work so hard for their families in their chosen fields that the actual family gets or feels lost and misses the point of their well-meaning efforts? Are these men, me included, missing the point? Was I substituting provision for real love and involvement? Had I crossed a point of no return? I feared my inability to connect with my family during the tragedy was going to cause an irreparable separation.

Why is it that we don't appreciate what we have until we face losing it?

At some point along this torturous cycle of questioning, I decided to retreat into the isolated wilderness further to insulate me from the ills of the outside world. I decided I would delay my return to California. In a week I would close down our fishing lodge at Lake Clark and relocate to my other lodge on the Holitna River, deep into remote Alaska. I knew that this decision exposed my inability in this crisis as a husband and was basically a cop-out.

In some ways, this decision helped me cope although I was still miserable. I started attending to the needs of closing the lodge immediately. Somehow, amid the busy work, the denial, and the pent-up frustration of the week, I was able to keep the guests laughing and to give them what they needed.

After our last great day of remote, fly-out fishing, my guests and I were on the flight back to the lodge. I was idly looking out the window and reflecting on the clouds that hung over the mountains—and over my marriage. I knew it would be two long months or more before I would see my wife. Would the rift be too wide by then to bridge?

The pilot made a beautiful landing on the lake and began taxiing the plane up to the lodge. My eyes drifted along the shoreline, and I saw a mirage of Sharon standing on the bank.

There, catching the sunlight with her blonde hair, was Sharon waving as smoke rose from the lodge behind her. It was just like before, before the tragedy of Elmer and our boating accident, before the emotional distance, before I had failed Sharon. I suppressed the hope that rose within me, shook my head and rubbed my eyes to release myself from this vision.

But when I reopened them, Sharon was still there.

I lost myself in a wave of disbelief and excitement, not knowing how I would approach her.

Sometimes I wish I had jumped out of the plane into the cold water, gone to her, and kissed her till she fainted. But that just isn't me. I was too stunned. Was I the first to get off the plane? Nope. Second? Nope. I was hiding. In the back. I was the last one to disembark. I was still in shock. I kept peeking out of the window at my wife. The pilot finally said with a chuckle, "Hey, Rock, I think someone is here to see you."

I slowly got off the plane. I saw a lot of people standing around and watching me. *Why don't they get a life?* I thought. I walked coolly up to my wife, and we just stood there looking at each other. I was so glad to see her that I was about to burst, and I wanted to tell her I was sorry, but I was too embarrassed to show it or to move any closer. She wasn't fooled, though. She could see it in my eyes. My happiness twinkled in their depths. She gently took my hand and squeezed it.

"What are you doing here?" I said dumbly.

"You didn't think I was going to give up on my man, did you?" she answered. "I'm never going to let you go."

Sharon, my best friend and the one who knows me better than any other person, understood the implications of my decision to retreat emotionally into the wilds of Alaska.

Wow! I knew as soon as I got her into my cabin and out of sight of all these gawkers, I wasn't going to let her go either! That night was one of the most special evenings we have ever had. We held each other and cried. We grieved over our loss and wept with happiness over our love. We shared a deep physical and emotional experience, strengthening our bond as Sharon and I both relived the last days of separation and difficulty. Sharon tenderly recalled the last conversation with her dad, the last he had with anyone. In the midst of all Sharon had been through, she chose to come to me. Her effort had a lasting impact on me and our marriage and gave me a deep belief in her commitment.

I realized that, in some ways, I had given myself to my mistress, Alaska. I had also succumbed to every man's temptation to provide things rather than love. I probably have one of the most masculine, prove-you-are-a-man jobs in the world. However, of all the things I have faced, commitment to my mate has given me the greatest challenges but has also been the most rewarding.

NINE

Baffling Bear

"Why did you come to Alaska to bear hunt?" I asked my contemplative guest. We had just flown into this remote ridge overlooking some marvelous valleys and streams, and I had set up a comfortable camp for this hunting combo. My guest sat in the tent in some ragged-looking, holey, rust-stained silk pajamas. You know what? Let's just call him Rusty. Rusty was tapping his finger against his leg, next to a rip in the seam. I know people get attached to things, but these pajamas had seen better days!

"Well," he drawled, "there are a couple of reasons." He paused, and I waited, curious to hear what he had to say and sensing it would be interesting.

I have learned that my guests come for many reasons, some strange, some obvious, and some downright funny. When I first started my business, I assumed what my clients really wanted was to catch lots of huge salmon and harvest trophy big-game animals. This couldn't have been further from the truth. That may have been what they *thought* they wanted, and for some that was a big part of it, but for most that wasn't the case. Some just needed to get away from whatever was pressing on them back home. Some sought serenity and wanted to experience a spiritual bond with nature. Others were trying to "find themselves" and needed this arena to search their souls. A few daredevils craved to push themselves to the limit and actually looked for life-threatening adventures, seeking to measure their manhood and see exactly what they were made of. Some may not have really wanted an Alaskan Adventure but had been pushed by friends or had won the trip at a fund-raiser.

And then there was Rusty.

"I see you have noticed my pajamas," he said. I nodded, a little sheepishly. "Well," says he, "if you've got a moment, I'll tell you a little story."

Hey, I was miles from nowhere. I had all day. These Southerners were always so polite!

"I reckon I do," I said, mimicking his accent.

"It happened awhile ago when these here pajamas were pretty new. I'd been married only a few years, and I gotta admit, I was getting a lil' restless. Even stopped goin' to hear that 'noyin' preacher." He paused and looked out the tent, seemingly searching his memory, then continued. "I wanted to go on this here fishin' trip with some of my buddies. Now, I ain't sayin' they were all men buddies, but I ain't sayin' they weren't either." He darted me a look, but I just nodded, so he went on. "Well, I tole my wife that I was goin' fishin' for a week at a cabin in the mountains with some buddies. I asked her to pack my new silk pajamas." He stopped again and began fiddling with his fingernails. I kept very quiet. I wasn't going to interfere with this story. He shook his head slowly as if remembering something that puzzled him. "My wife didn't say a thing, but I could tell somethin' was botherin' her."

"Well, I wuz all packed up, so off I go. She says to me as I leave,

'Have a good time, dear!' Now, that was kinda odd, her callin' me 'dear.'" (I wondered idly what she usually called him.)

As Rusty continued, his voice got quieter. I leaned in a bit closer to hear him. "Well, I gets back from this here fishin' trip, and when I arrive home, my wife is standin' in the doorway, wearin' my favorite blue print cotton dress and casually twirlin' my kid's baseball bat in her hands. She asks me sweetly, 'How was the fishin', dear?' I tole her the fishin' was jest fine and that we had fished ever' day, caught our limit, gone back to the cabin tuckered out, had a few beers, and slept hard all night. She was standin' real close to me and lookin' me directly in my face. I then remembered somethin' about the trip and asked her, 'Honey, how come you didn't pack my new silk pajamas?'" Here Rusty paused again. I was dying for him to finish his story.

It was probably only ten seconds, but it seemed like a full minute before he spoke again. He rubbed the side of his head, looked at me, and in a stronger voice, asked me, "Do you know what she said to me?" I had no clue, so I shook my head and waited. A faint grin crept onto his face, and he said, "She tole me that that was a very strange question for me to ask her, 'cause she *had* packed those silk pajamas—in my tackle box!"

I cracked up, laughing so hard that I nearly lost it. Rusty laughed right along with me.

When I recovered, I had to know. "What did she do, Rusty?" I asked.

He rubbed his head again and said, "She conked me with that bat!" (I couldn't resist looking at his head for confirmation.) "I was out cold for 'bout ten minutes, and when I come to, she is standin' over me with that bat gripped tight in both hands. She yells at me, 'It's about time you woke up! I didn't wanna hit you again till you was awake!'" We both started laughing again.

I then recalled what had started this conversation and asked, "How did that become the reason for your trip?"

Rusty chuckled and said, "Well, we made up, and I changed my ways. I knew right then and there that that little hellcat in the blue cotton dress was all the woman I would ever need. I took my silk pajamas out of that tackle box, removed all the hooks and rusty lures and sinkers stuck to 'em, and I've worn 'em every night since as a reminder of my special little woman, and to keep me from strayin'. This year is our twenty-fifth anniversary, and as a present to me she sent me on this trip! And you know what? She even packed my silk pajamas in my gun case!"

You might be surprised at the stories I hear. Some of them might even be true. Seriously, though, men often open up and tell me things they probably haven't told anyone for years, if ever. Ours is a healing environment. For the ladies out there, men really do want to talk; they just do it better in a fishing boat! Think about it.

The next morning it would be bear hunting time, and on the off chance that Rusty hadn't pulled my leg, I probably needed to provide some evidence that he had actually been hunting! Rusty and his friend, Dusty, were excited, but we hadn't seen any bear on the flight in, and they weren't fully convinced we were in the right place. I told them I could call up grizzly bears and had trained my voice to make a series of special calls that were irresistible to them. They both looked at me in disbelief, eyebrows raised. I observed this, rose to the bait, and said, "You know what? I'll just call 'em up right now, and there'll be grizzlies at our tent by morning!" We all laughed, but I was only half joking.

I went outside just before we went to bed and got ready to make my "grizzly calls." Electronic calling devices are not allowed in Alaska. I explained to Dusty and Rusty that each call represented a different element in the basic brutality of these powerful animals. The first call mimics the squealing of a small cub being mauled and killed by a boar (male) grizzly. The boar kills the cub so the mama bear (sow) is forced into heat sooner, since she no longer has a young one to care for. The second call mimics the screaming of the sow as her cub is being attacked. The third call mimics the grunting of the boar in foreplay. Learning these calls takes a lot of practice, but they are very effective if done well and can bring the entire grizzly family a-lookin'.

"Yeah, right!" Dusty said sarcastically after my explanation. Now I was being challenged! *All right, I'll show 'em!* I thought. I then began using my predator mouth call and making a series of grizzly calls. I spent some extra time and effort to really sell them. I knew that if there were any grizzlies within earshot, they would get curious. Dusty and Rusty got a big kick out of the calls.

Rusty said, "Heck, son, even if that don't work, it was still fun watching the show!"

We crawled into our sleeping bags and, as is my normal custom, I slept in all my clothes. I do this because it is about the only way to dry wet clothes without starting a fire. We hadn't started a fire, because that often spooks nearby animals. I unbuckled my belt, wiggled around to find the fewest number of bumps, and began to snooze.

I was fast asleep when, suddenly, I was being jerked and pulled. I came to with a start, and the first thing I saw was Rusty standing over me in his Skivvies—say, what happened to those silk pajamas?—and yelling, "Rocky, there's bears out there! Right outside! There's bears next to our tent! Look! Rocky! Rocky, get up! There's three *big bears!*"

I thought, *OK, he got me once, and now he's trying to do it again!* I wasn't going to bite. I said disgustedly, "Shut up, man! Don't be doing that to me!"

But he kept insisting. "No, Rock, I'm serious! I went outside to take a leak, and they scared me to death! They're right outside! Big bears! Look, *look*!" I did look—at him—and noticed his Skivvies were all askew, he was shaking, his shirt was sideways, and he had dirt and leaves on his shins and feet. Geez! Maybe he was telling the truth. I jumped up and scrambled to the tent door. I peered out and saw, not more than fifty yards away, three of the biggest grizzlies I had ever seen in one group. Two were eight-foot bears, and one was over nine feet. Wow!

Dusty and Rusty quickly and quietly put on their clothes and got their guns ready. I watched the bears, and they were milling about, in no hurry to leave. They kept looking over at the tent and sniffing the air. I could tell they were very curious. These were absolutely beautiful Toklat interior grizzly bears. Each had a different coloring.

We crawled quietly out of the tent, and Rusty and Dusty got set to shoot. They decided on which bear they each wanted, and it was agreed that Rusty would go first. He aimed carefully, and then, *bam*!

Suddenly, Rusty's "live target" turned and charged straight for him! Eight hundred pounds of muscle and fury, going all out!

I could not *believe* how cool this man was. He calmly took aim again at the oncoming predator and fired just one shot. That bear collapsed almost instantly about twenty-five yards away. Rusty's bullet had gone straight into the bear's mouth, clipping a tooth and striking the bear in the brain. The bear died on the spot and without pain. What an extraordinary shot!

Meanwhile, on the other side of me, it sounded like a war zone. *Bam! Bam! Bam! Bam! Bam! Bam!* Dusty was firing away at another bear that was fast getting "outta there" with his friend. I watched with increasing consternation as bullets hit the tundra everywhere but near the bear. Fifty yards in front of him, forty over and to the right, another way past, bullets were being sprayed everywhere!

When the bear was about three hundred yards away, though, one shot hit him. The bear stopped and began spinning around, snapping at its tail. Then he turned and disappeared into the alders.

Not again! Remember the code of Alaska? Always track a possibly wounded animal? I started out after the bear, yelling for the two men to follow. Since I was intently staring at the trail the bear took, so I could track him, I didn't bother to look back. I got to where the bear had entered the alders and yelled out, "OK, stay close behind me. Load up and be prepared to shoot in an instant if the bear rushes us!"

I didn't get a reply, so I turned around and looked for my companions. Great! They were running back to the tent as fast as they could go! How do you like that?

I felt a little let down but knew I had to find that grizzly, so I began searching carefully for any sign of blood. I finally found some small splotches about three feet high on the brush and alders. It was red and showed no white spots or flecks. I remembered the bear spinning and snapping at his tail and guessed that he had been stung in the rear end or hind leg. He had been moving fast when I last saw him, so if it was a leg shot, it was superficial. He had gotten nicked just enough to be mad and might be somewhere ahead waiting to ambush me! And I was in his backyard, on *his* turf.

Tracking is tedious work, and since the amount of blood I found was small and only in little streaks and droplets on the bushes, it was hard to follow. Also, it is absolutely amazing how many little red things there are when you are looking for something red—sage, berries, leaves, plants, my checkbook! I was focusing on my task pretty hard and had gotten fairly deep into the alders. It is easy to get lost and turned around in these mammoth patches of snarled limbs and leaves. Of course, this is home to the bears: their living room, kitchen, bathroom, and bedroom.

It has often amazed me how these big animals are so at home in such a congested environment and how easily they move about in it. Meanwhile, I was losing the trail and having plenty of difficulty moving freely.

Suddenly I came to a complete stop, and so did my heart. I heard a loud crashing noise, and then another, and the sounds were getting closer and closer! A large animal of some kind was crashing through the alders, right at me! I was in a tight spot in more ways than one.

I twisted around, facing the sounds, and steadied my .338 rifle. I was tired and tense and started shaking as the sounds became louder and louder. I could just see enough through the dimly lit alders to catch flashes of brown. Then I caught a glimpse of the head. It was a grizzly bear, headed right at me!

I knew I would only get one shot. I did not want a shaking hand for this encounter, so I grabbed an alder with my left hand and laid my gun's barrel across my left arm. I pointed it at the only spot between me and the bear that I thought might afford a decent shot. It was a small opening about eight feet away. The bear was now only fifteen or twenty feet from me and coming through heavy grass directly at that opening. I prepared to fire, hoping I wouldn't miss, because I knew I would only get one try!

All I could see was the bear's back as he prepared to exit the grass. I wanted to see his head before I shot, and I curled my finger around the trigger, ready to squeeze.

The grizzly did not come out roaring and snarling, ready to rip me to shreds, as I expected. Instead, he stopped, slid forward onto his chest into the clearing, spread his front legs out wide, and began whimpering like a dog! Needless to say, I was baffled at this bear!

In all my years of guiding and hunting, I had never seen a

grizzly act like this. He lay there for at least ten seconds, sniveling and rubbing his chin on the grass. He was directly in the clearing I was aiming at, only seven or eight feet away, and I had a clear shot, but I held my fire. This was not the same grizzly that I had been tracking. His coloring was much darker, and he was much smaller. The only way I can describe it is that this bear was acting like a whipped, cowed dog, head down, whimpering in front of its master.

I don't know if the bear got a good whiff of me—and after a few days in the wild, that lil' whiff can be deadly—but he got up, then slowly turned and ambled off into the brush. Your guess is as good as mine, but I gather that he may have thought I was his mama when he came running at me, realizing only at the last second that I was not.

I never did find the grizzly that had dodged Dusty's barrage of bullets, but I am sure that ten footer (they get bigger when you don't get 'em) will give hunting camps a wide berth in the future.

The next day, I called for my plane to search the area, but they couldn't locate that bear either. So Rusty packed his silk pajamas, and Dusty, his shooting medals, and we made it back to the lodge safely with a lot of laughs and a couple more grizzly bear yarns.

I think the biggest impact this adventure had on me was the realization that not all of our concerns are as real or as big as they may seem at first. Now when I become worried about looming trouble or some impending disaster or I listen to the fears of one of my children, I often reflect on how I felt as I heard that grizzly charging me in the alders. From the loud crash it made as it rambled through the bushes, it sounded like the "mother of all grizzlies." As I stood expecting the worst, I wondered what would be the outcome. Was this the end of the road for me? I was trapped with nowhere to run and no one to turn to, and I knew I was probably going to be killed.

Yet when the grizzly arrived and I faced him head-on, it was he who became afraid and submissive, not I. Why?

I believe it was God. He enables us to face what we greatly fear and will give us the strength to overcome that which intimidates us the most. That certainly has proven true for me.

TEN

Up in Smoke

I was going home!

My winter home is in Rocklin (even towns like my name!), California, about thirty miles east of Sacramento. It had been another season of unique adventures, but finally I had a moment to relax.

As I made my final preparations, I looked closely at my hands. There were nicks, dents, and numerous scars from thousands of hours of skinning animals, cleaning fish, clearing brush and trees, building my lodges, and a hundred other things in my profession that were rife with opportunities to cut or injure myself. I had taken advantage of many of those opportunities. Seeing all the calluses, scars, and bumps on my hands made me feel good, though. These were visible signs of my love for my family. I had gotten all these marks while doing my best to provide a good life for them. I was sure other men looked at themselves and their assorted physical marks similarly: mechanics with their grease and grime, farmers with leathery faces and gnarled fingers, accountants with ink stains and tired eyes, coal miners with blackened hair and skin, and so forth. Other professions create nicks, bruises, and wounds that are not visible but are just as relevant. Hospital workers, air traffic controllers, mothers, teachers, and a thousand other career people live under stress or deal with other challenges, leaving their marks in some fashion. All these are signs of love, whether visible or not, demonstrating efforts to provide. I thought of the hands of Jesus and the reasons for His scars. Those were the greatest signs of love ever displayed.

I wondered idly how often these very symbols of our diligence to support were treaded upon. "Don't you come in this house with those greasy hands!" Or, "Don't touch me with those dirty finger-nails!" And, "Your face and hands are getting old and wrinkled!" Or, "How come you're so tired all the time?" I chuckled to myself and thought, *Men are really pretty simple creatures. They are gatherers and do this to show their love and, yes, their manhood.* Well, I felt like a man today. The past season had been good, and my family would get some nice things. I was on my way home with the bacon. (OK, maybe it was silver salmon fillets and caribou sausage.)

I had just closed down my lodge and cabins, and no one would live there for over six months. My place would be snowed in, the nearby Holitna River frozen over, and the lodge almost impossible to get to during the worst part of winter. Temperatures would fall to forty below zero on a regular basis.

To prepare the lodge for winter, we would clean and lock all the cabins except one. On that one, we would leave a conspicuous note stating that it was free to use, especially in case of emergencies, but to please leave cut firewood and extra food if possible. This is another long-standing code in Alaska. Remote cabins are free to use for those who are lost or just need somewhere to stay for the night. But the rule is, leave them in better condition than you found them, cut firewood, and provide food and supplies, if possible, for the next desperate traveller. This has saved countless lives of those stranded in the wilds of Alaska. Recently a friend of mine and his wife crashed their plane and would have died had they not happened upon such a cabin in the middle of a blustery snowstorm.

I'm sure you have heard of some of the tremendous interior wildfires that occur in Alaska, covering thousands of acres and burning for months. The state of Alaska spends millions each year hiring anyone brave enough and tough enough to go out and fight many of these fires. But some are often in such remote areas that they are just left to burn. Because of these often uncontrolled fires, it is basically impossible to obtain fire insurance, especially on remote, unoccupied dwellings. Log cabins, woodstoves, and thick brush are a recipe for fire. Out-of-the-way cabins are made from local resources, so they mostly consist of wood. Each year as I left my lodge, I prayed that it would be there untouched upon my return.

A couple of years earlier I had been on a hunting trip, and as I was making my way back downriver to my lodge, I came across a couple of natives in a boat coming upriver. In a land where another human may seldom be seen, everyone who *is* seen becomes a friend. We stopped on the shore, chatted amicably, and I even offered them some cigars. As the pungent smoke drifted upward, one of the men said, "Say, there is a big fire a few miles downriver." I immediately felt my stomach lurch. My lodge was the only real lodge on the river for miles. He continued, "It's across from an orange buoy that is on the river."

Oh no! That was *my* orange buoy! It was my lodge!

I rushed downriver, and my fears were confirmed. The main cabin was ablaze.

What do we do in remote Alaska when there is a fire? There is no fire department to call. Instead, those brave enough to live along the river buy Honda water pumps that are placed in the water and attached to hoses, providing water to fight fires. That failing, we just grab any container, access the closest water source, and start a bucket brigade.

It was too late for my lodge. We used the pumps and everything we had, but it was gone. We only managed to save the outbuildings.

How had the fire started? One of my guides had gotten lazy, and instead of putting a small amount of kindling covered with cut logs, split in quarters or halves, into the woodstove, he had simply packed it full of kindling to make a quick, hot fire. He then lit it and went to sleep in another cabin. He got a hot fire, all right! By the time he awoke, the main lodge was fully engulfed.

It took two tough years to rebuild the lodge. I took what safety steps I could, flying in tin for the roof, installing a chimney fire arrestor, and putting in special stoves less likely to create a fire. I decided to go for broke. I built new cabins, a workshop, a sauna, a fuel shop, all within fifty yards of the river. In all, I wound up with eleven cabins and outbuildings and a new main lodge. Business had been good, and I wanted to give my guests the best accommodations I could afford. I spent over $600,000 to make it really special.

In my secluded area, everything has to be flown in with bush planes or rafted upriver from Sleetmute, adding to the already high cost of supplies. We cut and hewed our own timber, and the only electricity we had was provided by gas generators that were hauled in by boat. Gas had to be flown in for boats, planes, and the generator at four to six dollars a gallon. In the end, the effort was worth it. It turned out beautiful. I looked at my hands again. Those scars represented years of work, but now I had the lodge of my dreams. Now I could go to the next level in taking care of my family.

I had been very thorough in closing down my lodge. I dragged the boats far up the bank and turned them over. I hung up the motors in an outbuilding, drained them of water, and prepared them for winter. And finally, I gave all extra food and meat to my neighbors.

During hunting season some of my hunters give their animals to needy families via a transfer of possession form signed by the hunter. A government-sponsored program in Anchorage is in place to accomplish this. We donate heavily via the Alaska Fish and Game and often directly to needy villages. The villagers sign the proper forms and are given the meat. It is one way I try to give back to the land and the people that were there before us.

Interestingly, once, after I donated a nicely dressed caribou, the natives requested, by way of law enforcement, that I return many remote miles back to the kill site and get the heart and liver. They were upset when I didn't go, but the cost would have been exorbitant, and these items are not generally harvested, especially by nonnative hunters, nor are they required to be. That experience taught me that these items were a delicacy to the natives, and I was chagrined at the anger expressed when I did not comply and spend hundreds of dollars to retrieve them. Talk about an expensive slice of liver!

I also promote catch-and-release for all salmon. I call it my "playboy rule" and allow my fishermen to keep for personal use far less than the regulations allow them to have. Most are only too happy to oblige, and although we catch a lot of fish, most of these are released unharmed. We especially encourage catch-and-release for all native species of trout, char, grayling, and northern pike, particularly the larger fish. Fresh salmon is served at the lodge, and we allow a small box of fillets at the end of the week for the fishermen to take home, but the amount of fish actually caught and kept from the river system is relatively small. Of the few fish we do keep, we try to keep only the smaller males and not the hens, thus allowing the females to lay their eggs and promote good future salmon populations.

We have an association with a taxidermist who makes replica mounts. When someone catches a large fish he wants mounted, we simply measure, weigh, and photograph the fish then release it! The taxidermist makes a beautiful life-size mount almost indistinguishable from the real thing. In fact, I like the replica mounts better than skin mounts and am a big advocate of using them. They very accurately depict the fish right down to its individual markings and yet give the great feeling that the same fish remains wild and free. Replica mounts are becoming more and more popular and are easier to maintain. How nice not to have to deal with a smelly frozen fish and try to keep it somewhat fresh until you get it to the taxidermist!

I report to the Alaska Department of Fish and Game all unguided clients who keep more than their limit. Unguided clients are hard to monitor, but we tell them up front what the law is and what our policies are, and most are very cooperative. We want to preserve this beautiful land and its resources.

I reflected on the past season. What an interesting year it had been. During one week I had eight Mexicans from Monterey, ten Germans, and five Norwegians. The Mexicans would take a siesta at midday, have a fiesta till late at night, and sleep in late the next day. No matter what food they were served, they would supplement it with hot peppers and spices they had brought with them. The Germans were quite disciplined, went to bed early, and got up early. They ate a whole lot of meat. The Norwegians just went with the flow and had no inhibitions, often swimming in the cold river or lounging around the saunas totally nude. They were into a healthy diet, ate fish and organic foods, and loved power bars. Each culture was interesting to watch. Alaska itself is a melting pot of different nationalities, so the fifty-seven varieties of ethnic groups that visit each year seem to fit right in.

Two short flights and two long flights later, I was finally back home in Rocklin. Talk about culture shock! Suddenly it was so noisy! Everything is speeded up, and there are cars everywhere, concrete everywhere, music, video—and *so many people*, people who are not your friends and would be highly suspicious if you initiated a chat! I wonder if a prisoner goes through the same culture shock I did upon his release back into society. I had been a prisoner too, of the wilderness, sealed off by its vastness and silence. And the really strange thing is, once I got over the initial shock of coming back, it's as if I never returned. Everything was the same, as though I had been there all along and my absence never made a difference.

People don't realize how little they really matter to the regular pace of life. Leaving civilization is like removing your finger from a five-gallon pail of water. The little ripples close in behind you, the bucket of water becomes smooth and still, and in a matter of moments you can't tell your finger was ever there.

Things fall off of you in the wilderness, pace slows down, and stress disappears. There are no packed freeways, drive-by shootings, negative news stories, horns blasting, road rage, endless lights, pavement everywhere, or paper, paper, paper! Even the smells of society are absent: gas, oil, perfume, garbage, soap, smoking brakes. There is a realization of how unimportant and silly some aspects of life can be.

I leave California in May, return in October, and the same talking heads are wagging on meaninglessly. News anchors are still creating and gleefully reporting dissention, and so-called experts are fussing endlessly over fashion changes. I didn't hear about the O. J. Simpson murder trial for months after that whole fiasco, and when I returned, people were astounded that we didn't know the story. But I'm not sure I miss out on much each year. Sports are the only thing I actually miss. Sometimes people bring newspapers. Interestingly, in that environment they read like fiction. Then I wake up to reality each day in Alaska and face adventure and nature. It never ceases to amaze me how quiet the dangerous wilds of Alaska are and, conversely, how noisy our "peaceful" society is.

There is a saying, "Our wants are many, but our needs are few." In the wild there are few choices to meet one's needs: hunt, fish, eat, sleep. Yet back in the Lower 48, the number of choices is overwhelming: ads, clothes, movies, restaurants, hotels, recreation, computers, Internet, TV channels, events, games, friends, and enemies, to name a few. In society, animals are no longer your neighbors, but a different kind of wolf or shark may be lurking nearby.

Well, at least I have six months of new movies to watch each year!

I was finally home, and I'll bet you can't guess the very first thing I do each year when I get home. Haircut? Shave my scruffy beard? A long, hot shower? Take my honey out to a fabulous restaurant? Nope! I go to McDonald's! Big Mac and fries! And man, do they taste good!

A couple weeks and a few Big Macs later, I got the call—the call that curdled my blood and chilled my soul. A pilot friend of mine, Henry Hill, had flown over my lodge in Alaska and had seen smoke. He flew lower and confirmed that it was burning. My new, beautiful lodge was on fire!

Henry is a pilot out of Sleetmute who delivers supplies, grunts, and an occasional smile all over that region. He has a voice that sounds like Sean Connery's. "Rocky," he said when I answered the phone, "I've got some bad news. Somebody is burning down your lodge."

I answered numbly and in disbelief, "You mean my main lodge is burning?"

"No, Rock," he replied. "*All* the buildings are burning!"

"That's impossible. How could they *all* be burning? Was there a forest fire?"

Henry answered, "No. It was arson. Rock, someone set all the buildings on fire."

I was in complete shock. My lodge, the eleven cabins, and all the outbuildings were on fire. And I was thousands of miles away and helpless to stop it! My life, my business, my world, all going *up in smoke*!

What could I do? I had no fire insurance on any of the property. I had spent every spare nickel and then some to rebuild my dream lodge. And I already had people booked for the following season. How could I hunt or fish with them now? What about their deposits? What about my wife and girls?

I called the Alaskan state troopers, and they were very honest with me: "Not much we can do, Rock. She'll just burn herself out. We'll go take a look and see what we can find, and we'll do what we can, but these types of crimes are hard to pin down."

Their investigation revealed that three Alaskan citizens were likely involved. They had taken a boat upriver to my lodge, broken into my toolshed, gotten axes, and busted down every door. Then they took gas from my fuel cabin and poured it everywhere. They also tied rags onto the ends of a couple of fishing poles and doused them with the gas. They lighted these and then used the extended poles to light every cabin, outbuilding, and then the main lodge on fire. As if that weren't bad enough, they also saturated the boats and motors with gas, set fire to them, and shot them full of bullet holes. They hated either me or my profession.

I was devastated. I moped around the house for a few days not knowing what to do. I kept thinking that I had to go and do *something*! Doing nothing was driving me crazy.

Henry kept me updated. He told me the fire had burned so hot that it had even gone underground into the tundra, becoming a fire that would not go out. It burned for weeks, in fact, even after the area was covered with snow. It had gotten into the peat underground, and since the soil is porous enough to provide oxygen, it smoldered and burned slowly, like a hot oven. Next it moved along the peat and got into the root system of the trees. After getting into a root system, a fire will gain momentum and finally erupt into flames again, destroying the support system of these trees and causing them to fall, tumbling haphazardly everywhere. This was happening all over my property, and the smoke was oozing up from the tundra and snow. It created an eerie, surreal, ghostly sight, like a deadly game of blackened Pick-Up Sticks.

Suddenly I had the thread of an idea. Would it work? It was a crazy, harebrained thought, but I was a man of action, maybe even reaction, and to sit still was to die inside. I had to go.

I bolted like a startled rabbit. I was out the door and on my way to my lodge to try and recover something from the ashes, maybe even to create magic out of smoke and mirrors. I'll be honest, my hopes were mostly wisps of smoke, but it was better than what I saw when I looked in the mirror: a man who was doing nothing while his livelihood was at stake.

I landed in Anchorage then caught a long flight to Sleetmute, which is thirty-six river miles downriver from my lodge. (A good rule of thumb for "river miles" is that for a typical winding river, three or four miles of river equal about one mile by air or in straight line.)

When I arrived, I began negotiating with a local resident for the loan of his snowmobile. That little chat lightened my load a hundred dollars, but soon I was off, zipping up the frozen Holitna River to save my lodge, even if I had to do it with my bare hands! The wind blew cold on my face, but I knew I was soon to face the far colder possibilities of my family's future.

It was midday, but the distant sun provided no warmth. Suddenly I caught a brief glimpse of something dark just ahead. Instinctively I swerved violently to the right and crashed sideways into the snowy bank of the river. I crawled up, shook the snow and ice off my face and clothes, and looked back at the dark object. It was a hole in the ice. I had just missed going headfirst into the frozen river. I never would have had a chance.

I climbed back on the snowmobile and warily continued down the dangerous snake of a river. I was beginning to get very chilled, even through my snowmobile suit. The wind was beginning to pick up, and I realized I had no water and little food. And how far does a snowmobile go on a tank of gas, by the way?

After several hours I made it to the lodge, and the scene was right out of a horror movie. I expected Freddy and Jason to pop up any minute. It is hard to describe the devastation. It was far worse than I had imagined. The fire was still burning underground, and I could see wisps of smoke drifting up through the moss and snow into the chilly air. Charred trees lay strewn about, and the whole place smelled like badly burnt toast.

It was difficult to traverse even a few feet, because the fire had gutted certain areas, leaving deep pits and holes. I learned this the hard way, falling almost twelve feet through an upper crust of snow into smoke and nearly frozen mud.

It took me several long minutes to claw my way out, and I was only successful due to some roots I found and grabbed near the rim. The dichotomy between tremendous heat and Alaskan cold was hard to register mentally, as was the complete destruction before me.

I finally came to a complete stop and let the whole scene sink in. I gritted my teeth as I looked at my dream lodge, gutted, blackened, and sideways; cabins and outbuildings the same; huge trees, fallen and lying crisscross atop them; boats and motors piled up, charred and burnt, full of holes, and resembling something out of a junkyard. It was a total loss, and even worse, it could not be repaired. Nothing could be rebuilt here. I had spent $600,000, and all I had to show for it was a $140,000 still-active note on a charred, worthless, smelly barbecue pit.

If the reason for burning my lodge was to preserve nature, it had backfired. More natural resources had been destroyed permanently than ever would have been saved. I don't know how many hours I searched for something to salvage, but I began to feel foolish and helpless. I was also beginning to chill—on the outside *and* on the inside. I was hungry and thirsty. I gobbled some snow for moisture and ate a sandwich and candy bar I had brought along. The candy was frozen and hard to bite into. And I was suddenly very tired.

I climbed under an overturned boat that was above a still-burning area of tundra. The heat felt great for a few minutes until the smoke seeping through began to suffocate me. I knew that if I fell asleep, I would die from smoke inhalation. I couldn't believe that there was nowhere here for me to find shelter, garner some heat, sleep, and survive. All of my buildings were gone. I had not prepared for this. It was now close to 10:00 p.m., very dark, and thirty-six windy, cold, icy river miles back to Sleetmute. I knew in my gut I would not make it all the way back. I would be frozen stiff before I got even halfway. I also knew I wouldn't make it here either, in this graveyard of dreams.

I then remembered my silly idea. It seemed even sillier now as I stood alone, freezing to death and miles from nowhere. I remembered a loner sourdough and his wife who lived in a homemade cabin eight miles up the river. Would they be there now? If not, would I be able to break into their cabin and survive?

I had to hurry. I had tarried far too long, consumed with my loss. I jumped on the snowmobile and started upriver by moonlight, praying that I would not hit any patches of open water. I could feel the core of my body slowly going cold. My hands, ears, and feet were numb. I raced through the dark, snowy night, hoping the sputtering snowmobile would not quit.

I wasn't sure, but after a while I thought I could see just a tuft of smoke from up the river. Was I dreaming? Maybe they were there! Only a mile to a warm cabin. *Come on!* I told myself. *Focus! Don't fall asleep! That is the lure of the Ice Maiden calling! You're tired, Rocky. Just lay your head down on my lap for a while. Go to sleeeeeep. No! Don't listen to her! Don't quit! Don't stop! Keep going! Don't close your eyes!*

I hardly remember arriving at the cabin. I jolted to a stop and fell sideways off the snowmobile, hitting the icy surface hard. Startled, I grabbed the side of the snowmobile and dragged myself up. I started staggering toward the cabin door and could see drafts of light filtering out from the window. I hoped that what I was seeing was real and not a cruel dream or the Ice Maiden trying to fool me again. *Keep moving!*

Now, please understand that I must have looked like some type of humanized grizzly. I had windblown, flowing, frostbitten hair and beard; wild-looking, lost eyes; a K-Mart snowsuit bundled about my substantial frame; and of course, I was sporting my naturally lovable teddy-bear face. Imagine this: It's near midnight in the middle of absolute Vacantville; a blizzard is howling outside; and you, the crazy occupants of this remote cabin, are sure you have *not* invited anyone over for dinner. In fact, you have not seen another human, besides your mate, for a couple of months and don't expect to for months to come! The closest town is a roadless forty-four river miles away. But suddenly someone or some*thing* is banging away at your door!

Looking back, I am surprised I wasn't shot. I must have been quite a sight. I stood there trembling, bent over, barely able to stand, and smacking away with both arms on that door as hard as I could.

Someone hollered loudly through the door, "Who are you?"

I said, "Sam, it's Rocky. I need your help! I'm freezing to death!"

Sam opened the door a wee crack and peered out at me. After a long pause, he said forcefully, "I didn't do it, Rock!"

Huh? What . . . huh? I was trying to register what he had said, but he continued.

"Rock, I didn't burn your place down! I didn't do it!" He opened the door a little more.

I looked at him with wild, uncomprehending eyes and said, "Sam, I'd like a cup of coffee." He didn't respond, so I said, "Sam, I can't make it back. I gotta stay here tonight."

He frowned, looked at my hands carefully (probably checking to see if I had any weapons), and then grudgingly stepped back and mumbled, "Well, OK. Better come in out of the cold."

Ahhh! Warmth at last.

My reception from Sam's wife, Pam, however, wasn't warm. She looked at me and pointed to a framed picture prominently displayed on a homemade hutch. It was a lovely photo of their recently deceased sixteen-year-old son. Putting her hands on her hips and glaring at me, she said, "Let me tell you something, Rocky. You can replace your lodge. You can build a new one, but I will *never* get my son back!"

Stung by her rebuke, I stumbled to the couch and sat as close to their lifesaving, hot, crackling, burning woodstove as I could. It's ironic how fire can bring either life or death. Hours before, I had viewed its destruction of my lodge; now it was giving me comfort and healing. I could feel the life and energy inch their way agonizingly back into my body. I held the proffered coffee with both hands because I couldn't have done it with one. It was several minutes before I could manage a sip with any degree of safety. I think it was the best cup of coffee I ever drank.

We talked until pretty late. When I had somewhat regained my faculties, I said, "Sam how much money do you have in your pocket?"

He looked at me, startled, apparently saw I meant no harm, and replied in a low but firm voice, "Rock, I don't even have to look. We've got very little money to our name!"

I looked over at Pam and saw that her face, which had been drawn, and her eyes, which had appeared tired and sad, now perked up. My question had piqued her interest. I continued with mounting confidence. "Sam, I am in trouble and looking to make you a deal you can't refuse!" No one spoke. I waited a moment, glanced at his wife, and said, "I want to rebuild my lodge right here!" With that, I pulled a check out of my pocket and asked for a pen. I placed the check in front of me on an empty chair so all could see and slowly wrote on the amount line, "Fifteen thousand dollars." I then wrote on the memo line, "5% down payment on Holitna property." I watched Pam as her eyes lit up and her back straightened. I saw Sam's eyes widen as he stared at the check now lying face-up on the chair. His mind was racing and quickly computing my offer of $300,000. My future now lay on that chair. I waited anxiously for the verdict.

The next morning I became the new owner of their land and cabins. I hired Sam to help rebuild some outbuildings and do some upgrades. He did a wonderful job! Sam and Pam left the next spring with a big return on their odd investment. We had both gotten a new start. And due to continuing faith in me from close friends and my family, I was able to completely rebuild a new Holitna Lodge and even add some cabins on the property. It is where I operate today. With a lot of work, the willingness to take a gamble, and some divine guidance and forbearance, broken dreams can be rebuilt.

Reputations are critical in Alaska. It is a huge state, but word travels like a juicy rumor in a small town. I repaid the $140,000 loan that I owed on the burned-out property. The previous owner was dumbfounded. He fully expected me to default and return to him unusable land. Maybe someday I will be able to find a way to make that property beautiful and useful again. You never know what can happen in the unpredictable wilds of Alaska. But meanwhile, my reputation had been saved.

It has been rough making a comeback after such a huge setback. I had faced the death of my business. But at least there is hope. Where there is hope, there is will, and where there is will, there is almost always a way.

After much discussion with my wife and a lot of prayer, we determined to show goodwill and not pursue the investigation or press charges. This is not some fluffy, heartless response either. We had lost a lot but had learned and gained a lot too. In these situations, you can't replace what you've lost. The only thing in your control is your response, your attitude. We hope our response will go a long way toward showing that we are not only good stewards of the land but also good neighbors as well.

ELEVEN

Alaskan 9/11

The sun was just peeking over the rolling hills of the misty marsh, and a cool breeze was bathing my face in wonderful smells. I watched spellbound as a very special moose, his massive antlers dripping early-morning dew, resolutely stomped toward me. As he got closer and closer, I froze. I could not move! I could only stare at this mammoth moose that I had tracked for years. He kept on coming right at me, his big, round, brown eyes never leaving mine. It was the largest moose I had ever seen.

Since I was only here on a scouting mission, I'd had no reason to purchase a tag, so I could not shoot a moose. And suddenly I knew that he knew it! He was the smartest moose I had ever hunted. He knew I could not shoot him! I could see it in his eyes. How had he figured it out? And what was he going to do?

Slowly he came. Ten yards away . . . five. Then he stopped directly in front of me, his face within inches of mine. His hot breath blew on my cheeks, and his long tongue dangled to one side.

Suddenly, he began talking to me! "Rocky! Rocky! Get up! Are you going to sleep all day?" I groggily came to. Where was I? Another crazy dream!

Roscoe is an exceptional moose that I have attempted to harvest several times over the years. He had become such a legend to me that he had infiltrated my dreams. Taunting me while I hunt, taunting me while I sleep. He was probably tucked away safely in his valley, laughing at me right then. Many of my clients have sought this esteemed creature, wanting the trophy rack that his keen wit has kept alive and growing throughout the years. I decided this year would be different. He was mine! We would see who would be laughing then!

During one of my scouting flights several years ago, I found a remote valley that I instinctively knew would abound with trophy game. There is just the right cover of alders, the right steepness of the surrounding mountains, and plenty of water and food supplies. It is an Alaskan haven. And Roscoe is its centerpiece.

My client then had been Norm Hahn, a devout Amish man who is a fabulous cabinetmaker. In fact, he is the president and chief executive of Conestoga Woods Specialties, a large, internationally renowned company. He had signed up for a combination black bear and moose hunt.

The only landing place we could find for my bush plane anywhere near the secluded valley was a couple of miles away on a tricky ridge. We managed the landing, set up camp, and started out on our hunt the next day. Norm was in good shape, and we finally reached a nice knoll overlooking the valley.

That's when I first saw *him*. I immediately felt I was in the presence of a king.

In the middle of the valley was the biggest moose I had ever seen. His colossal horns were gleaming in the dawn. In keeping with his size and prowess, he had a big harem of cows around him.

Norm and I stood there gaping. We were both excited. The moose was over five hundred yards away, so we carefully scoped the surrounding terrain and planned our stalk. We would have to be careful not to spook any of the cows around him.

We had just begun our stalk when suddenly, out of a group of alder bushes not seventy-five yards from us stepped another big bull moose. His rack was well over sixty inches, and normally he would have been a real prize, but I knew the first bull we had seen had antlers over seventy inches. I whispered to Norm, "Norm, don't shoot this bull. I want that seventy incher!"

Norm looked at me and very calmly in his Amish way said, "Rock, what the Lord giveth to me, I will take. A moose in the bush is better than a moose in the meadow." I blinked, trying to digest his words. The other moose was only four hundred yards away and preoccupied with his girlfriends. We had a chance to get one of the biggest ever harvested in that area!

"Norm," I said, "let's go for the other bull; he's not that far away!"

Norm shook his head slowly and said firmly, "What the Lord giveth to me, I will take!"

Norm took careful aim and shot the nearby moose cleanly. I was shaking my head in disbelief, but Norm's words and actions have returned to me often. The prize that so many have sought (and I've even dreamed about!) was easily passed over by this man. He knew his priorities, that's for sure. I've often recollected Norm's cool dismissal of something that would have caused so many other hunters to drool. The shot would have been so easy to make! But passing it over was an act of someone aiming for a different mark.

As it turned out, the moose rack Norm did get measured an awesome sixty-three inches, and Norm even harvested a trophy black bear the same day. He was thrilled with the moose he chose, and I bet it tasted great to his family throughout the year. And at least I knew where "my" moose was, and he wasn't going anywhere. I vowed to return. That was when I gave him his moniker—"Roscoe."

Roscoe had picked the perfect valley, though, for safety. It had many good hiding places, impassible beaver dams and ponds, and lots of soggy tundra, making the going near impossible for hunters and predators. Surrounding this valley were canyons and difficult terrain, with no place to land a plane for nearby access. It was a beautiful, pristine valley that I had dubbed "Virgin Valley."

After my hunt with Norm, I excitedly told the famous evangelist Franklin Graham, son of the even more famous evangelist Billy Graham, about Roscoe. Franklin wanted a chance to match his wit with the moose's and win himself a trophy rack like no other. Franklin is a great friend of mine, so I told him where Roscoe was, some tips on how to hunt him, and where he could try to land. I also cautioned him that Roscoe was a hardened reprobate, had little use for preachers, and would resist any invitation to Franklin's table. Franklin is a wonderful pilot and managed to land his plane on the narrow ridge I had previously scouted. Unfortunately Roscoe was not in the mood to be sacrificed on the altar just yet and turned a deaf ear to the word and "calls" of the evangelist. Aye, this fella Roscoe was indeed a willful beast, and it was going to take much prayer, faith, and fasting to bring him to his knees.

After my efforts with Norm and Franklin to get Roscoe, that rascal became a master of hide-and-seek. I think he took great pride in confounding us.

Several years passed, and Roscoe outwitted all. It would take someone in good shape with a good shot and a lot of patience to get him, and I knew just the guy—Ron Smalling, a doctor friend of mine from Missouri. He had a very busy medical practice, so he was sure to have a lot of patience—er, I mean *patients*!

After the 2000 hunting season, I went to visit Ron. He works as an interventional cardiologist—don't ask me what they really do. All I know is that these heart doctors save your life, and then when you get the bill, you have another heart attack! It's a revolving door!

Ron had hunted with me before and looked forward to his trips to Alaska to get away from the high stress of his profession and enjoy an adventure. We were in the trophy room of his beautiful house in Branson. This room was dedicated to North American animals, and there was an empty spot above the fireplace being saved for a big moose mount. It was to be the centerpiece of his collection. I said, "Ron, Roscoe would really look good up there!" I could see the gleam in Ron's eyes. He wanted that moose too.

For the rest of that year he looked forward to his quest to get Roscoe. He shared his dream with friends and patients, even some conscious ones. I am sure he daydreamed about it during quiet moments. Ron called me often and was obsessed with this hunt. He could hardly wait to get started. He could visualize the mount on his wall above the fireplace. His hunt was scheduled to begin Monday, September 10, 2001.

Sunday, September 9, finally arrived, the day before the start of the big hunt! Ron and I were at the Holitna Lodge making final preparations. He was nervous and excited.

My pilot, Joel, ferried us out and made perfect landings on that risky ridge near Virgin Valley. We set up camp, checked out the area, and chatted. A beautiful black bear watched us from about two hundred yards away. Ron wanted a black bear and had gotten the appropriate tag, but due to the "fair chase" rule wasn't allowed to hunt until the next morning. Of course the next day that bear was long gone! He kept up with the law too!

"I saw a grizzly in the valley on the flight in," I told Ron, "and it's the first time I've seen one there. I don't know what effect that may have on Roscoe, but we'll have to hope for the best. If we do get a moose, we'll have to watch our backs, especially at the kill site. Grizzlies and black bears both love moose meat."

I've often heard it said that grizzlies and black bears will not inhabit the same area. This is simply not the case. A grizzly can and will kill a black bear, but they still feed in the same berry patches. I have frequently observed both grizzlies and black bears in close proximity, thus totally contradicting the myth.

Ron was getting really pumped up about his hunt the next morning. I wondered if he would be able to sleep. I could hear him tossing around in his sleeping bag all night.

September 10 dawned clear, chilly, and damp. We arose at 5:00 a.m., while it was still dark, in order to get to the valley before daybreak.

Upon exiting the tent, Ron exclaimed, "Look at the thousands of stars in the sky!" On clear nights in Alaska, the stars are so numerous and distinct that their brilliance produces a heavenly light show with each star glistening like a diamond. You almost sense that you can reach out and grab a handful. It was a gorgeous start to a fateful week in history.

We began our hike to the valley, traversing some steep slopes and being careful not to silhouette ourselves on ridges. It was strenuous work, and Ron was breathing hard. I pushed him to keep up, knowing we only had a small window of time. Finally, we reached a great overlook with good cover and were able to sit and glass the valley. Ron had been sweating, and it was cold. I could see that he was shivering and pale. I knew if we sat for a few moments he would get his wind back, and the rising sun would begin to warm us up. I began looking through my binoculars for Roscoe.

I had seen Roscoe before in the near side of this valley, and this was the only place we could set up a stalk. The far side of the valley was almost impregnable; if he was there, we would not be able to hunt him. If we even tried and somehow scored on a long-range shot, it would still be nigh to impossible to get to him, and totally so to pack him out. I carefully scanned all the nearby areas of the valley. No Roscoe. I scanned farther and . . . there! I saw him! It was Roscoe, harem intact! But he was at least a thousand yards away and on the other side of the valley. Either the grizzly I had seen or our plane landing the day before had spooked him.

"What a bummer!" I said to Ron. "That rascal is onto something! Well, let's just watch and see if there are any other moose in this valley. I have seen several big ones besides Roscoe." I continued to watch for other moose but kept an eye on Roscoe. He kept moving farther away. I wanted to shout at him, "Come out and play, big guy!" I could tell Ron was disappointed too. He kept looking down at his feet and then staring wistfully in Roscoe's direction.

Ah! There! I spotted three more bull moose, heads down, locking horns and obviously in full rut. They had nice racks, too, two of them fifty inches plus. One looked close to sixty. "They look good," I told Ron. "Let's go for it!"

A fifty-inch moose rack is a huge rack. Many lifetime Alaskans have never harvested an animal that large. By regulation, nonresident moose hunters are not required to have a registered Alaskan guide with them. However, to reduce out-of-state harvest, the state of Alaska requires that any moose shot by a nonresident must have a minimum antler spread of fifty inches, or it must qualify under a couple of other tough criteria. Alaska rightfully defines any moose rack over fifty inches a trophy animal.

We began our stalk, and I searched for a knoll overlooking the meadow, but the moose kept edging away from us, so I finally settled on a spot about six hundred yards downwind from them. I could not tell if the one I could now see was the sixty incher or the fifty-plus incher I had seen earlier, but I thought this one might be the bigger of the two. Ron set up shooting sticks to put his rifle on, and I hid in the alders to try to "call" the moose in. I figured that all three moose were still within "calling" distance. Whichever responded to my moose calls and came to us was the one for Ron.

I cut a stout piece of alder and began beating the brush with it, simulating the thrashing and rattling antlers of a challenging moose in rut. I intermittently made robust bull moose grunts, imitating one bull challenging another to a fight over a cow (some things never change!). I interspersed these sounds with low bleating cow calls, emulating a cow moose wooing her intended. Of course, this makes the other bulls jealous—oh my, the trouble these ladies lead us into! My cow calls sound eerily like the bawls of the farm cows I used to hear as a young boy on my grandma's place in Mississippi.

It worked. The moose stopped, perked up his head, and did some thrashing of his own. He then began edging his way toward us.

Ron was using a range finder that could accurately read distance. The moose was cautious and easing toward us slowly. At about 380 yards the moose stopped and turned sideways. He wasn't acting too eager to come much closer. I asked Ron, "Are you comfortable enough to take him at this range?"

Ron nodded quickly and said, "Yes!"

"Go for it!"

Ron took his time and squeezed off a shot. I could tell by the dull thud that he had hit the moose. He shot again, and the moose went down hard.

Moose are the largest antlered animals in North America. The largest of them can weigh near two thousand pounds. This fella was probably close to fifteen hundred. The fun was over, and now the work would begin.

When we got to him, he was already dead. I am always happy to see that, because I hate to see any animal suffer. I was proud of Ron and his shooting. Initially he was excited too.

We did a quick measurement of the horns, and they turned out to be fifty-three inches. As this dawned on Ron, I could see his enthusiasm fading. He had dreamed for a whole year of Roscoe and that seventy-inch-plus mount above his fireplace. He had traveled far and was confident he would succeed. Well, Roscoe was alive and well, and tauntingly out of reach. Instead, Ron had this beautiful but smaller rack.

I reflected back to the many times as a youngster that my two brothers and I had dreamed of getting a fifty-inch moose rack. Although we grew up in Alaska and hunted for years, I was the only one who succeeded in doing that.

I knew better than to intrude on Ron's thoughts. So Jared, an assistant guide, pilot, and packer, and I began caping and processing the moose.

After a while we got tired, and I said to Jared, "Hey, let's take a lil' break!" I can sleep anywhere, anytime, bear country or not, and I promptly laid back and went sound asleep. Jared did the same. Ron told me later, "I was so surprised. I heard snoring, and when I turned around to look, you and Jared were fast asleep!" He said he was thinking, *My master guide is asleep in the middle of nowhere, next to a bloody moose kill, without a care in the world, even though he knows a huge grizzly is in the area! He already warned me that grizzlies love moose meat and will fight over a kill site.* "Bugs and mosquitoes were zooming around my head," he said, "and fear was racing through my heart." So . . . he got his gun, chambered a round, and kept a sharp nervous lookout.

After almost an hour, I woke up refreshed and continued with the moose. I glanced at Ron and saw that his head was down and his face was slack. He wasn't saying much. I felt bad for him and said, "I'm sorry we didn't get the one you wanted." Ron nodded and looked away. I thought of my Amish friend, Norm, and continued, "Ron, this is the moose that God wanted us to take today, for reasons that we don't know."

The pack would be horrendous. First we would have to traverse out of the valley, over tundra and creeks, through alders and brush, then up a steep canyon and down another slippery slope to our camp and landing strip a couple of miles away. Each pack would be 150- to 200- plus pounds. I knew Jared needed help, so I decided to call in another packer, Jon, who is also my gourmet cook. I got on the phone to my pilot, Joel, and told him to fly Jon in and then me back out to the lodge.

"I'll be back tomorrow," I told Ron when Joel and Jon arrived. "In the meantime, Jared can help you hunt for a bear or a wolf. If I were you, I would set up on the kill site." Little did I know that by early morning the next day, no private planes would be flying anytime soon. Ron, Jared, and Jon would be on their own, without communication or supplies from anyone for days.

Joel flew me back to the lodge, then refueled and flew to another airfield near his home so he could be with his family. I did some chores, called my wife, and slept soundly.

The next morning was Tuesday, September 11, 2001, the day when cowardly men—religious zealots—using civilian planes as suicide bombers, crashed into the Twin Towers in New York and the Pentagon, killing thousands of innocent people.

I was up early that historic Tuesday morning and was stunned when, over my shortwave radio, I began hearing snatches of news of the terrible terrorist attack. I immediately called Sharon, who was back at our home in California watching the horrific events unfold on TV. She was crying and in shock. It is still hard to comprehend even as I write this. Misguided religious zeal has caused untold harm throughout history.

The FAA grounded all domestic planes indefinitely, including my plane. No guides or pilots in Alaska were able to fly and thus were powerless to check on the hundreds of hunters stranded in remote field camps. A fortunate few who could be reached by river or all-terrain vehicles were contacted and rescued.

One pilot friend of mine tried desperately to fly in supplies to a hunter he knew was low on food and water. He was forced down by military F-14 fighter planes. He said their meaning was very clear when they showed him their trigger fingers, followed by a thumbs-down sign. He didn't even have to know any military codes. This was a national crisis and way beyond serious, but here in Alaska our hunters were in serious peril too.

Meanwhile, Ron, Jared, and Jon spent Monday night, September 10, at the field camp and had a great time talking about the bear and wolves they had seen and the moose that Ron had shot.

The next morning, Jon and Jared continued to pack out the moose meat. During one pack, they observed a grizzly and a couple of wolves. They reported this to Ron, and he carefully sneaked up on the kill site, hoping to get a shot at one of the wolves.

Ron got within 150 yards of the site. Later he described to me what he saw: "Rock, I witnessed something I thought I would never see. A huge grizzly was sitting on the moose carcass surrounded by three Alaskan timber wolves. More unforgettable was that one wolf was white, one tan, and one black. It was a surrealistic scene: three wolves, casually sitting no more than twenty yards away from that big grizzly bear, spread out in a semicircle around him.

"A few moments later, as if on signal, the three wolves got up and began to purposefully circle the bear. They were trying to intimidate him! Well, it worked. The bear got nervous, backed away, and hurried off into the bushes. The wolves then descended on the kill, eating ravenously." When Ron told me this, I reflected back to the city of Jericho and how the Israelites had circled it for seven days and accomplished the very same thing.

Ron had hoped to harvest a couple of the beautiful wolves, but before he could set up to shoot, something spooked them and they bolted. He didn't get his wolf, but he did get to witness something that was, to him, simply remarkable.

Ron, Jon, and Jared had fully expected me back that afternoon, or at least by evening. When I didn't show, they began to worry. They knew that I was reliable when I made plans and that only if the weather was bad or something serious happened would I fail to show. Since the weather was good, they were concerned that I had crashed. There is an old saying in the Alaskan wild, "If nobody is flying, somebody is dying." Something devastating had happened, all right, but since I could not communicate with them, they were clueless about the horrendous events going on far away from their field camp.

Their fear became stronger and stronger as each day passed without me showing up. In Ron's own words, "We formulated all kinds of possibilities, thinking the most likely was that the Super Cub had experienced mechanical failure, but we also entertained the very real possibility of something drastic, like a crash. In fact, that became a more worrisome and likely possibility, since no one came out to our hunting spot and we were quite sure Rocky would at least send somebody to fly over and check on us. We had this horrible, ill feeling that there was something wrong but did not understand it."

I was going crazy back at the lodge. I knew that my friends had a reasonable amount of supplies; some water, with more available in a nearby creek; and, of course, plenty of food, especially considering all the moose meat. But every guide worries about his clients, and I was feeling truly helpless, not being able to check on them.

I did a lot of cooking at the lodge for those pilots that would no doubt be stopping at my private airstrip—no others were available for miles—and to keep busy. I also continued listening in fascination to the reports on the radio, as well as to those I received from Sharon and from Joel. I called Ron's family and assured them he was OK. As soon as we were allowed to fly, I told them, I would send my satellite phone with the pilot so Ron could call them the moment my plane reached his camp.

Many pilots and guides began pressuring the state of Alaska about their many clients stranded in the remote wilds. In some cases of dire emergency, the state had to respond to rescue hunters. The FAA Web site reported that as many as eight hundred people were stranded in rural Alaska, some without any knowledge of why they had been abandoned. Frantic calls came in to the FAA about marooned hunters, permission for medevac flights, and ferrying aircraft out of the state before the winter weather. Air traffic employees at Anchorage Center worked with North American Aerospace Defense to authorize individual medical flights, including one organ transport. I heard reports that one hunter died, but I have not been able to confirm this.

Finally, at first light on September 13, we were released to fly. I immediately sent Joel to Ron's camp. My friends were thrilled to see my plane approaching them, but they were also upset that no one had been there for days.

Ron stomped over to Joel after he landed. "Where have you been?" he blustered. "Where is Rocky? Why hasn't he been back out here to hunt with me?"

Joel answered in a quiet voice, "The United States has just faced a major terrorist attack."

Ron thought Joel was jerking his chain. He looked hard at Joel, but when he realized Joel wasn't smiling, he said, "What are you talking about?"

"On Tuesday morning," Joel responded soberly, "several civilian planes were hijacked by terrorists. They purposely crashed them directly into each of the Twin Towers in New York and another into the Pentagon. The Twin Towers collapsed, and thousands of people have been killed. All civilian planes were immediately grounded until this morning."

Ron knew it was no joke. He then began to fear for his family. "I gotta get back to the lodge ASAP," he said, "so I can call my wife!"

"Here, call her right now!" Joel said, handing Ron the satellite phone and assuring him that I had kept his family informed in his absence. Ron was joyous to learn his family was OK and thrilled to be talking to his wife. He told her he loved her and would be home as soon as he could get there.

Ron wrote to me later:

I will never forget landing on the dirt runway behind the Holitna Lodge, taxiing up to the lodge, and seeing your smiling, bearded face as you greeted the plane. I got out of the plane, embraced you, and felt tremendous relief that we were all okay. You recapped the events as you understood them from 9/11 to 9/13. You told me it was the first time since the beginning of airplane flight in America that all flights had been halted nationwide for so long. I will always remember the next words you spoke to me. You looked up into the sky and said, "Ron, God is in control, not me. We may not understand these events, but God sees the past, present, and future, and He is in charge. We must trust Him."

It took Ron three long days to get from Anchorage, Alaska, to Springfield, Missouri. Getting anywhere by plane or car was almost impossible during that time. Airports and borders were packed. Thousands of Alaskans tried to drive the Alcan by personal, rented, or borrowed cars and had a terrible time with snowy, congested roads and closed borders. When Ron was finally able to hug his wife on September 16, it was a special moment of pure joy.

I remember where I was when I heard about Kennedy being shot, Armstrong landing on the moon, Boston winning the World Series, Grenada being attacked, Iraq being struck, Ali (Cassius Clay, then) winning the heavyweight championship, and the U.S. hockey team winning the Olympic gold. Now I would forever remember where I stood on 9/11/2001. Events such as these redefine our lives and the way we see our world.

Ron wrote this about the impact his adventure had on him:

After I got home, the days and weeks passed, and I reflected on my adventure. Pretty soon I realized that that 53" moose was a trophy of a lifetime, and the events surrounding that hunting trip had changed my life forever. I then understood Rocky's words in the field when he said that was the moose that God had intended for me to have. I understood what that meant now. I began to become more deeply appreciative of the wonderful gifts of life, health, loving family, and my ministry to others in my work as a cardiologist. That spurred a reevaluation of my life and my purpose, which began to draw me closer and closer to

God. Ironically, I used to feel that I was so vulnerable when I was out in the Alaskan wilderness. I viewed the United States as a relatively safe place. Since these events, that concept has been reversed. The Alaskan wild with all its wolves, grizzlies, cold weather, and hardships is much safer than our "civilized" world.

I agree with Ron. Alaska is God's special land of healing for those who open up their minds and hearts to its extraordinary touch. I have discovered that if I learn to accept even some of the hard things God brings my way, though I may not understand the purpose at the time, I will usually learn from them later—and grow.

TWELVE

Run, Baby, Run!

I was standing in my Zodiac inflatable raft, unmindful of the risk of capsizing, and screaming at the top of my voice, "Run! Run! Run, baby, run!" The guy in the boat with me was waving his arms frantically and yelling, "Go! Hurry! *Run!*" Two groups of men on opposite shores were shouting, jumping up and down, and screaming, "Run! Get! Don't stop! Please, baby! Run!" A cacophony of earsplitting sounds knifed through the cold air as we all stood transfixed by the scene unfolding before us.

Have you ever had those dreams in which you are being chased and your legs are not responding? Have you ever felt that life is pressing down on you and if you stumble, you will be swallowed alive? Is there a "grizzly bear" of fear or worry or financial failure nipping at your heels? If so, you will relate to this story. It is an amazing tale of an actual run for life. It is a story of a mother's struggle to save the life of her young. And this was not a dream; it was a nightmare in progress.

Every ten years or so, someone is born with a voice that must have once been an angel's. When you hear the pure tones and sweet sounds, it captivates you and may even bring tears to your eyes. Something beautiful often has a magical effect on us. Well, there is a place nestled in Lake Clark National Park that has this same type of surreal beauty and impact.

Lake Kontrashibuna (easy for you to say) is a pristine, seventeen-mile-long, gin-clear lake, high in the mountains and surrounded by peaks. It is cold and very deep in spots, having been carved out by huge glaciers for thousands of years. At the upper end is a mammoth glacier that feeds the lake. At the lower end, the spectacular Tanalian waterfall cascades down through huge rocks, forming the source of the Tanalian River.

Due to its location and configuration, only two game fish, lake trout and arctic char, inhabit the lake, with no access for others. The few feeder creeks along the sides of the lake bring only small bait fish and clear snowmelt. Little char get eaten by bigger char, these char get eaten by even bigger char, and the large lake trout eat anything smaller than themselves. These fish grow to mammoth size, and we have caught lake trout up to thirty-three pounds and thirty-seven inches. Some of these denizens of the deep are probably close to thirty years old. Their average growth rate is one and a half inches a year. I became so enamored with the lake and its beauty that after a couple years of fishing there, I enforced my playboy rule, "catch and release," and required all anglers to use barbless hooks. Only if a fish was foul-hooked to the point it could not live would I use it as additional delicious fare in our shore lunches.

I liked to take clients there on a day trip during the middle of the week, and it was intriguing to watch their transformation as they leisurely spent a few hours in this paradise. Clients who had fished nonstop from dawn to dusk on previous days would set down their poles, find a comfortable spot to relax, and simply soak in the majestic scenery. Intensity and stress would peel off of them like skin from a molting snake, promoting rejuvenation. It wouldn't take long for the stillness to seep into their souls. It was a magical place, and my guests often told me it was their favorite fly-out trip of the whole week.

Flying there was tricky at times because the wind could come up in a hurry in this canyonlike, long, narrow finger of a lake, preventing our 1954 DeHaviland pontoon-equipped Otter from taking off. There is an old saying about the wind: "Wind from the east will blow three days at least, and the third day will be worse than the first!" It is uncanny how accurate this often proved to be. So if we saw the afternoon wind beginning to mount, we would get everyone together and leave immediately. Once my assistant guides weren't quick enough, and the party was stuck there for three days. We had to air-drop supplies to them.

On this particular day at Lake Kontrashibuna, I flew in my clients, split them into two groups, and put them on opposite shores of the lake. One group was on a small strip of sandy beach a couple miles up from the falls, near a feeder creek next to an old trapper's cabin. The cabin is well constructed and fascinating to explore. A little creek runs through a sluice and directly under the cabin. This and several other cabins are preserved as historical buildings.

I ferried the other group a half mile to the opposite shore, past an island, to another gorgeous spot. It was a simply beautiful Alaskan day. I was in my Zodiac, and one client wanted to fish from the raft with me.

My client and I were motoring along contentedly on a slow troll toward the falls, about three hundred yards up the lake from the island and the two groups of fishermen. Something caught my eye, and I looked up the mountainside, far above the trapper cabin, and saw a cow moose running along the mountain, about a thousand yards away. She was angling down toward the lake, traversing meadows lined with small, sparse spruce trees. A huge grizzly bear was chasing her. I said to my friend, "Hey, look at that moose. She is being chased by a grizzly. It's all right; he doesn't have a chance. She'll outrun him in no time." We both watched the spectacle of beast against beast with interest.

But as I continued to watch, I became puzzled. The moose was not running as fast as I knew she could, and the grizzly was not giving up. He maintained a steady, loping pace about twenty to thirty yards behind her. After a few moments, the moose turned and headed directly at the lake. She still did not increase her pace much. I was confused. What was she doing? Why was she only going at half speed? Was she injured?

What is that phrase? "Out of your depth?" Moose use water for safety against bears and wolves. The long legs of the moose allow them to keep contact with the bottom of a lake or river a couple feet deeper than the grizzlies and wolves. Once the moose reach this depth, they will turn on their predator, rear up on their hind legs, and begin kicking at them with their front hooves. I've seen it, and it is awesome to behold. The front hooves of a moose, horse, donkey, caribou, elk, farm cow, all can be deadly. I read recently of a donkey that killed a mountain lion with its front hooves, in full view of a hiking party. I told my friend, "That moose is headed for the lake, and after entering the water she will turn and attack the grizzly!"

The group on the moose and grizzly's side of the lake did not have a good line of sight and would not be able to see the chase, but I knew the group on the opposite shore could. I yelled at them and finally got their attention. After I waved and pointed frantically for a few moments, I could see them scrambling for cameras and binoculars. Meanwhile, I was still intrigued by the tactics of the moose. Why was she running so slowly, allowing the bear to keep up the chase?

This continued for the next couple of minutes as we watched spellbound. Finally, the moose reached the shoreline about three hundred yards up the lake from my group near the trapper cabin. I said, "Now she can run into the lake, set him up, and turn the tables."

But the moose did *not* enter the water. Instead, she began sprinting along the sandy shoreline, directly toward my group of fishermen! But that was not all.

I suddenly realized why she had not been running fast and felt a sharp streak of fear hit my gut. For the first time, I now saw a little calf running just to the rear of the cow, almost between her hind legs. My friend saw it too. We exclaimed, almost in unison, "Oh no! She has a calf!" Then I became fearful for my group of fishermen. The moose, calf, and grizzly were running straight at them!

I fired up my Zodiac and tried to race down the lake to warn them. The animals were running faster than my raft could travel, though, and I was losing ground. I could see my group, and when I got to within about two hundred yards, I began screaming at them, flailing my arms like a frightened chicken flapping its wings. They had no clue what I was trying to convey to them. They just stood and stared. The shoreline jutted out between them and the animals in such a way that they could not, and would not, even become aware of the danger until the animals were upon them. I felt powerless. I had no idea what would happen.

I watched as the moose, calf, and grizzly rounded the bend and bore down upon my clients. The grizzly was about twenty yards behind the calf. Then I heard screaming from those in my group and saw them scatter, poles flying everywhere. (I learned later that one pole had a fish on it, and that fish dragged the pole all over the beach.)

The moose and calf burst right past the startled crowd and then into the creek. The grizzly paused, but only momentarily. Mother and baby then ran into the lake and began swimming straight across. The grizzly now angled into the water, taking the shortcut toward its prey. I saw that some of my clients were on their knees— one had fallen—and they were all staring in disbelief at the scene before them. I heard one yell, "Go, baby! Go!"

It was then that I became aware of the noises the animals were making. The calf was bleating in a high-pitched voice, a terrifying sound. The bear was grunting in a low growl, and the cow moose was only occasionally answering her calf in a moderate bawl. They continued to swim toward the middle of the lake, the cow leading the way, the calf tucked close behind her, and the grizzly another ten to fifteen yards back.

The swimming animals created three Vs in the calm lake, each representing its maker, each unique, and each pointing to a struggle for life. The cow moose was making a fairly large V with smooth, consistent waves flaring out. The calf made a tiny V with small ripples, back of and inside the larger V of its mother, a graphic picture of a mother's protection. The grizzly was pounding the water with his front paws in a powerful breast stroke, and his huge head disappeared beneath the surface with each cycle of strokes. His rear feet were kicking in a froglike fashion. His V was uneven, with much larger waves, wiping out the other two Vs.

The animals crossed in front of my raft and were about a hundred yards away. They were headed toward the tip of the island, where I thought they would wind up. I found myself, along with everyone else, yelling encouragement at the calf: "Hurry, baby, hurry! Swim faster! Keep up with your mom! Go! Go!" We had all become cheerleaders, compelled by the struggle for survival happening right before our eyes. Each time the calf slipped back a few feet from her mom, our screams would increase and become more urgent. It seemed to help, or the calf would sense the grizzly getting closer and strain harder to keep up with her mom. How long could this little creature fight for its life? I could not believe how far this chase had already lasted. What could I do?

I knew I could not interfere. I had to keep my Zodiac raft far enough away to not disturb this violent drama. I wanted to take out my handgun and try to scare off the grizzly or, failing that, to shoot him. I wanted to help that calf! This rugged land, though, has it rules, its tragedies, and its triumphs. There are strict laws about improperly disrupting the course of nature, and this is especially true in Alaska state parks. It was not my place or right to intervene. I was invited by fate to be a passive spectator only. I just gritted my teeth, watched intensely, and prayed.

The creatures reached the tip of the island, and I was startled to see the cow and calf fly right past it. They now headed for the far shore. I realized now that the fishermen on that side had also become cheerleaders. They, too, had a clear view and were shouting at the calf. The calf was tiring and slipping back more and more often. Each time, we would shriek at her, and somehow the calf managed to find the strength to catch up to her mom again.

At last they reached the far shore. Maybe the cow moose would turn on the grizzly before he got his feet grounded on the bottom. "Get him, Mom! Turn on him!" I yelled.

But the cow did not turn on the grizzly and instead exited the lake. Then she trotted a few yards onto the shore and stopped. I was horrified. *Why did she stop?* The calf came out of the water, stumbled up behind her mother, and stopped too. I couldn't believe it!

"Run, run!" we all roared! The grizzly was only four or five seconds away from land. Why were they standing still? "Run, little baby!" I bellowed.

The cow moose looked totally exhausted. Her head was down, tongue hanging out, and she was unstable on her feet. She was breathing heavily, creating huge billows of frosty breath in the air. The calf was tottering too, also breathing heavily. The cow then looked directly in our direction, and I promise you, she seemed to be pleading for help. She was at the end of her rope, had no more strength, and was trying to let us know it. My heart went out to her, and I felt so helpless. The little calf was only a couple of feet high and mostly legs. I guessed it to be about three weeks old. Then I saw the grizzly, powerful muscles rippling beneath his wet coat, exit the water, and I knew this calf was not going to get any older.

Our yells were getting weaker, and a sense of despair was enveloping us all. "Don't give up! You can do it . . ." I heard my voice trailing off, and I watched in dismay as the grizzly charged the motionless calf. The cow moose instinctively trotted a few yards off and stopped again. The calf did not move. She just bleated, in shrill wails that sounded like a rabbit being killed by a coyote. The grizzly pounced on the calf and ferociously bit its neck and within moments picked it up with its powerful jaws and carried it off into the bushes. The calf continued to scream for a few seconds; then all was quiet.

The cow moose just stood there shaking as she witnessed her calf being killed. Afterward, she waited a few moments and then reentered the water. I watched her swim out to the island and lie down. How she had the strength to swim out there, I don't know. But she slept all afternoon and was still there when we left for the day. It probably wasn't her first experience losing a calf and, sadly, will probably not be her last. Our moose calf population is getting slaughtered.

A recent field test was conducted in our area by Alaskan wildlife biologists, who tagged 101 moose calves. All were eaten by predators; there were *no* survivors. At this rate, our moose population will not rebound for at least seventy years. It is becoming rare to even find a bull moose track. The Alaska Department of Fish and Game have told me privately that they estimate up to 40 percent are eaten by wolves and 50 to 60 percent by black and grizzly bears. Normally, when the predator's food source is low, it reduces the number of predators. This isn't true with moose calves and their predators, though, because wolves, wolverines, coyotes, and bears have numerous other food sources. Moose and caribou calves are a bonus, a delicacy, but not a necessity.

We should be good caretakers of our "garden," as Adam and Eve were of theirs. I believe strongly in "creation conservation," which involves pruning to make it more fruitful and reducing that which destroys the balance when necessary. I shake my head at the irony of how the predatory animal groups are the protected ones, defended to a point above and beyond all logic, at least to those who live in the wild and understand its true balances. The Alaskan moose is the premier animal in the North. It is a true treasure, but it is being destroyed, not by men, but by four-legged killers and well-meaning but misguided concepts. In the last few years, I have observed mostly old bulls and cows, with fewer and fewer young moose to take their place. I dearly hope that something will be done soon to correct this before it is too late.

This "adventure" impacted my whole group immensely. They could not stop talking about it for the rest of the week. For me, watching a predator devour the young and innocent was a powerful illustration of the devastation of our own youth by predators far more subtle but just as deadly. I wanted to go home and hug my four daughters. I wanted to tell them I would be there for them. I wanted to protect them and, beyond that, find ways to help all in our society who are vulnerable and defenseless. Many in my group felt the same way, and from such small beginnings as these are often born lasting ideas that benefit all society.

THIRTEEN

Disarming Dave

During my many years as a guide, I have often seen amazing healing through adventure. The following story is one of both tragedy and triumph. It is about an all-star professional baseball pitcher, a World Series champion, and a true warrior: Dave Dravecky.

In Dravecky's book, *Comeback*, Chuck Swindoll wrote the following:

> Dave Dravecky's story is not just another athlete's story, because Dave is not just another athlete. His major struggles have not been limited to locker rooms and pitcher's mounds.
>
> And though he has known the thrill of playing a vital role on a championship major league baseball team, his greatest victories have not been won in public ballparks. His most significant conquests have come deep within his own life as he refused to surrender to the same enemies that plague us all: fear and disappointment, pain and death.

Dave Dravecky related the following to me after his first trip to Alaska:

My arm and shoulder were amputated on June 18, 1991. That day, all control over my future, my security, my identity—everything—felt like it had been surgically removed along with my pitching arm. The macho "I-can-handle-anything" athlete was now an amputee. Was there a big *A* on my forehead? What was next? All I could do was pray that God would somehow show Himself.

Two months later, a friend asked me to join him for a weeklong trip to Alaska with some "famous Alaskan guide" named Rocky McElveen, who owned hunting and fishing lodges in Alaska. Man, I hit that offer with the hungry enthusiasm of an Arctic char lunging after a mouth-watering egg fly pattern! But in my condition, it wasn't the lure of Alaska's world-class fishing and hunting that hooked me. It was a way to test my abilities, both physically and mentally. I did not even know if I could shoot a gun or cast a fishing line or how, with only one arm, to fight a salmon once hooked. I could fail or be laughed at secretly as a cripple. I knew instinctively though that through adventure I could test myself and begin restoration of my manhood. This was a chance for me to face real challenges in the wilderness of Alaska. It was the chance to be alone, just God and me, face-to-face in an unhurried place known as "the last frontier."

I had watched this amazing athlete try to cope, not only with the complete amputation of his main arm and shoulder and the loss of his career, but also with the perceived loss of his stature as a man. He wrestled with not being whole, with painful emotions in his big heart, with phantom pain in his absent arm, and with the fear of not being able to provide for those he loved. He had previously come up for a fishing trip and proved he could catch fish. That marked the beginning of his restoration as a man. During that trip he and I had bonded deeply, and I was delighted to see him healing, but on this hunting trip I was going to push him a lot harder. No squirming salmon here. We were going for caribou.

We headed out to the Taylor Mountains with a couple of other famous friends. One was Don Dewitt, whom we called "Mr. Turkey" because he at one time owned the largest turkey farms in America. The other was Bob Knepper, another all-star baseball pitcher, at that time with the Houston Astros. As you might expect, there was a good deal of ribbing going on—professional athletes are especially adept at this. At dinner, I was sitting to Dave's left and joined right in with the jabs:

"Hey, Dave, could you give me some more elbow room?"

"Rock, Rock, Rock," he replied, in a wounded voice, but with a big grin.

Nope, no mercy here! And to Don Dewitt, "Sure, Mr. Turkey, you provide thousands of turkeys for others, but can you get a caribou for yourself?"

I have a special gun that is very accurate. It is a .338 necked down to a .30 cal rifle, and this baby is great at long range. Only a few were made, and I was trying to pitch this rifle to Dravecky. I said, "Dave, if we can figure a way for you to aim and shoot this gun, I can get you a caribou and maybe next year a bear."

"Nah," he replied, "I got this 30-06 hunting rifle, and I'm going to use it." So I got a long bipod, and we figured out a way for Dave to hold his gun with his one arm, allowing the front of the barrel to rest on the bipod. By tilting the bipod so it was now on only one leg, Dave could then shuffle to one side or the other to aim the gun at a moving target. It looked a little awkward to me, so I wasn't too hopeful Dave could hit anything in motion. He *might* succeed if it were standing stock-still.

For practice, Dave sat in the tent and shot at a rock about two hundred yards off. And you know what? He missed it, of course. Well, maybe he hit it once or twice. Not only did Dave have to compensate for the loss of an arm and shoulder, but he had to use his off arm to hold the gun and his off eye to sight and aim. He explained to me that his balance was difficult to relearn because the weight on one side was now greater than the other, and there was no arm to balance on his left side. What is our instinct when we lean one way? Stick out an arm or leg the opposite way. Consider the problems a guy on a high wire would have with only half a balance pole, and that usable on only one side. He'd better use a safety net! So you understand Dave's quandary.

We were camped out on Rifle Ridge. Alaska is a realm with no landmarks, at least no man-made ones. Out here there are no roads, no signs, and no way to be sure. So how did I know this was Rifle Ridge? I had named it, of course. How do I name locations? Well, in this case I had previously flown over this ridge, and as I looked out of the plane window, scouting for game, I saw that my new rifle had slipped out of its scabbard, which was secured to the wing struts. The rifle was barely hanging on by a single leather strap and was swaying wildly in the wind. I certainly couldn't get out and get it and was sure it was going to fall. I stared at that dangling rifle and felt a kindred spirit. I often felt I was hanging on for dear life too. But guess what? That rifle made it. We landed on that ridge, and miraculously the rifle remained attached and undamaged. And that's how it goes. Hence, Rifle Ridge. (A moniker often reveals interesting bits of history.)

Nightfall came, and we talked and then slept uneasily, waiting for the next day when we could hunt. I kept dreaming of Dave, spinning around his bipod, firing off shots like a machine gun mowing down batters wearing camos.

Yikes! I needed some coffee! I got up early, got everything ready, and set out hunting with Dave.

Caribou are migratory and are on the move at this time of year. Dave and I were on a slope and spotted a herd about three hundred yards away. They were upwind from us and, though they seemed to have seen us, could not get our scent. The cows circled one way, and three big bulls circled the other. (In the animal world, the female of the species often goes out to investigate whether it is safe for the male to follow. Whatever happened to that great concept?)

I set up the bipod, and Dave positioned his gun and got ready. Caribou have a "safety zone" of about 100 to 125 yards, meaning that unless something spooks them, they feel comfortable with potential trouble at that distance, but not much closer. The bigger bulls have a larger safety zone. If they can't smell you, they like to circle and get downwind. The three bulls were slowly circling us. They were also getting closer and closer. I told Dave, "When they get to 150 yards, shoot!" Dave grunted in agreement, and I saw that he was standing rigidly, with the gun on the now-one-legged bipod, allowing him to carefully pivot around the bipod, swing the gun, and follow the caribou.

One bull was particularly distinctive, with beautiful markings and a massive rack. I pointed him out to Dave and said, "Dave, let's take that one!" I then began counting down the yards for him: "250 . . . 225 . . ." I spoke more quietly as the caribou became more cautious: ". . . 200 . . ." At this distance they were becoming anxious and starting to move more quickly. At 175 I said firmly, "Get ready, Dave!" Finally, they were about 150 yards and beginning to trot. Dave was going to have to shoot at them while they were trotting. "Shoot 'em, Dave, shoot 'em!" I had hardly spoken the words when *boom!* the gun blasted off. I watched the big bull closely. He didn't even flinch at first, but boy, did they all bolt!

It was a clean miss, and now they were headed away in a dead run, precluding a second shot by Dave, who was unable to reload quickly enough. I urgently asked him, "You want me to help you shoot, Dave? I'll help you aim."

Dave replied angrily, "You better not help me! I don't need your help, Rock!" I moved a bit closer, just in case. "Get back!" he said firmly. "You better not help me, Rock!"

I backed up and shrugged. "OK, Dave, you're the boss."

I looked at the retreating caribou. I felt bad that Dave had missed but was secretly proud that he was tackling this without my help— and doing it his own way. He was determined to be his own man.

I took out my binoculars and glassed some more hills. Hot dog! I spotted another group of caribou. "Let's go after them!" I said. I noticed that Dave was fiddling with the gun and trying different ways to reload faster.

We got downwind from the caribou and, using the terrain and ridgelines, began our stalk. The caribou, however, had been spooked by the earlier gunshot, and we were unable to get any closer than 350 yards. They were staying on high slopes where they had lots of space and visibility. I said, "Dave, I'm sorry, but this is as close as we're gonna get. You'll have to try a long shot."

Once again he set up his new rig. I kept an eye on the caribou and let Dave make his own preparations. This time he also made arrangements to reload quickly. He was ready but would have to shoot soon. The caribou were starting to drift away.

Boom! Boom! The caribou jumped and fled, and I kid you not, they were laughing as they went! *Boom! Boom! Boom!* It was like the Fourth of July! The caribou just kept on going, unharmed. But I was really impressed at how fast Dave had developed the technique of reloading and firing again. This guy had a short learning curve.

We sat down and took a short break. I knew not to try to console Dave, but I could tell he was down.

We had only been seated for ten or fifteen minutes when suddenly Bob Knepper came running up and screaming at us. What was he saying? Had someone been hurt? Had Dave shot in the direction of the camp by mistake?

"How many d'you wanna shoot!" I finally heard him say. "What are you doing, Dave? How many do you want?"

Huh? What was Bob talking about? He kept shouting until he got right on top of us, then stopped and looked at us, obviously demanding an answer. Dave and I looked at each other, trying to figure this out. "Bob," I finally asked, "what are you talking about?"

"Don and I were sitting at the camp," he answered, "and about thirty minutes ago heard you shoot. We looked in that direction and saw three bull caribou come running over a ridge parallel to the campsite. We kept watching and noticed that the largest one started to falter. He went down into a valley, fell down, and died. So . . . how many caribou do you wanna shoot?"

Amazed, we hustled back to the fallen caribou, and lo and behold, it was the very first bull that Dave had shot at. We could tell by the horns and distinctive markings. Dave's shot had critically wounded the animal, but he had somehow run out of sight without showing the effects. He died within a few hundred yards.

It was about a mile to the camp, but it was a joyous mile as we processed and packed out the beautiful animal. Dave kept saying, "Yeah, you thought I missed, but I knew! I knew! That's why I didn't really aim the second time! I didn't want to shoot more than my limit!"

Yeah, Dave! You rock!

I could not get over it. This shot would have been very tough even for a skilled marksman with two arms and using his good eye. On Dave's first shot from a makeshift bipod, with his off arm and off eye, he had harvested a running caribou at over 150 yards with a rifle he had rarely, if ever, used. I knew I would never hear the end of it.

I reflected on how Dave had shot at this animal up close and it had seemingly gotten away. He had also experienced the best of life up close, and it had been taken away. The caribou, though, had not really gotten away, and I knew that Dave's heart, spirit, and life had not gotten away either. He was going to be OK. He had hit the mark in more ways than one. He had left one scene but would find greater achievement in another.

The next year, Dave was back. Over the years Dave has hunted and fished with me almost a dozen times. The week before this bear hunt, we spent fishing with some of our special friends. Among them was Chuck Swindoll, pastor, author, and the real definition of an encourager. Swindoll truly exudes adventure. All week he had been pumping Dave to go bear hunting. He kept telling him, "You can do it Dave! Go for it!" By week's end, Dave was primed and ready to go. I desperately wanted him to experience getting a bear. "Dave," I said, "if you get a bear, it could very well become an Alaskan Adventures record bear—in the one-armed man category!"

"Rock, Rock, Rock," he replied in that now-familiar wounded voice.

I had the special .30-378 rifle all set up for Dave and a shorter bipod that I hoped would be more stable and easier to aim.

We flew into Grizzly Ridge, and, yes, I named that one too. It should be obvious why it has that name. The name became prophetic to the clients who have hunted there. Well, it was a quiet camp that night, but I slept fitfully because of some crazy dreams. Maybe I should start having tea in the evening . . .

The next morning we awoke to sheeting rain and patchy fog. It was hard to see very far, and I knew hunting would be very difficult. I went up the hillside to a ridgeline to scope things out but saw nothing. So we relaxed, found a good viewpoint, sat down for a while, and began glassing slopes whenever the holes in the fog would allow. I then spotted a bear about 750 yards away across an almost impassable canyon. I knew our pickings were slim at best in this weather, and Dave is always on a tight schedule. So I said the first thing that popped into my head: "Dave, let's go get 'im!"

After only a couple hundred yards, I knew it was useless. First, the bear was only of medium size and not worth the trouble it would take. Second, he was on the other side of the wide canyon, and getting to him at all would be tough. It was basically senseless to expect to get close enough for a good shot without alerting him. So I stopped and said sarcastically, "Dave, let's just shoot 'im from here!" I thought, *This will be fun! And Dave will get some practice with that gun.*

Dave picked up on my sarcasm, lifted his chin slightly, and replied, "Just how far away is he, Rocky?" Ah, these athletes! Always up for a challenge. Maybe it is just the way we men are.

I said, "OK, big boy! You *really* gonna shoot from here?"

Dave quietly repeated his question: "How far is he, Rock?"

I decided to go along since I had started this. "Oh, he's over 500 yards if he's a foot!" I really had no idea how far the bear was, and I suspected he may even be over 600 yards away. But this was getting interesting. I did have a quick vision of Dave shooting that moving caribou on the last trip from about 150 yards, but I dismissed that as divine intervention. This bear was safe. Not only was he miles away, but it was hard even to see him through the fog. I didn't want that horrible pack anyway, but I said, "Go for it, big boy!"

Dave shot me a look and said, "OK, wise guy, I'll do it!"

I watched Dave load three shells, lie down on the ground, and carefully arrange his bipod. I helped him set up and tried to keep from chuckling as he got ready. I then lay on my stomach, parallel to Dave and his gun. I could hear Dave mumbling to himself, and it was clear he was mentally judging the distance, wind, etc., and trying to compute the required rifle elevation. Trying to suppress a grin, I said, "Go ahead, Dave. Take 'im!" When I got no reply, I stole a quick peek at Dave. Man, this guy was focused! His face was scrunched up, all serious, and he was straining to sight with his right eye, gripping the gun tightly with his right hand. He kept wiggling around to get situated just right.

Figuring he was about to pull the trigger, I turned my attention back to the bear and got ready to laugh. I noted that the bear was perilously close to a steep ravine just below him. I watched intently for the bullet to strike the hillside, raising a cloud of dust. I covered my ears tightly and waited.

I reflected on just how amazing professional athletes are and what nerves of steel they have. I especially admire the hand-eye coordination of pitchers. They don't "fever up" under intense pressure, with huge crowds screaming for them and at them. They are able to shut out everything and focus on the finest detail.

I was used to out-of-shape executives who had similar control over their minds but not their bodies. Dave had faced the crowds, pitched in the World Series, and won, but he was not an experienced hunter. However, I had seen that he had tremendous control over his body, his eyes, and his remaining arm and hand, even though it wasn't his strong arm or hand. Well, this would be interesting to see.

I continued to watch carefully, waiting patiently for Dave to shoot. Thirty seconds passed, then forty. Finally, I took my hands off my ears and was about to turn to see what Dave was doing when *ka-blam*! I had forgotten how loud that gun was. The explosion nearly knocked me sideways, and my ears started ringing.

In spite of that, I kept my focus on the bear. I realized in amazement that Dave had almost hit him. Was he going to kill this bear? I saw a small puff of dust erupt on the slope just above the bear; the bullet's path had been only inches—or less—above him. Since the bullet had struck beyond the bear and was traveling faster than the speed of sound, the bear heard it hit the ground behind him before the sound of the actual gunshot reached him. He was very confused. Frightening sounds were coming at him from opposite directions. He jumped and looked around. He even started toward us a few feet then stopped. He rose up, bobbing his head and nose up and down, trying to smell where the danger was.

Dave meanwhile was sighting in for his second shot. This time I put my fingers deep into my ears and kept them there. I watched dumbfounded as Dave carefully aimed again, completely controlling his mental and physical capacities.

Boom! The bear bounced upward and then fell into the canyon. I had never seen anything like it. No client with whom I had ever hunted had shot an animal from that far away, and yet this man, who had lost his best arm and shoulder not that long ago, had just accomplished it!

Oops! Now I had to go *find* that bear, and this was not going to be easy. He had fallen down a steep incline loaded with brush and alders. I carefully marked the spot where he had tumbled into the canyon; then we made the arduous pack to that spot. Down our slope, into the canyon, over several creeks and knolls, and finally up the far slope to where the bear had fallen. Our best estimate was that the straight-line distance from where Dave had shot was well over 600 yards.

Finally, we were in the right spot, but we could not find the bear. I knew I had to track him into the alders, but I wasn't in the mood to go into that thick brush after a wounded bear by myself. I pulled out my pistol and said to Dave, "Hey, hold this, will ya? Follow me and back me up."

You know what he said to me? "Rock, I ain't going in there! Have you forgotten, dude? I only got one arm!"

How do you like that? Like having both arms would make a difference in close quarters with a wounded bear! Athletes and their paybacks! He flashed me a big grin, sat down with a smug look, and got ready to watch *me* go get the bear.

I searched and searched but did not find blood. I did find fresh bear scat, which is a common sign when an animal is hit, so I knew I was in the right area. I bowed my head and prayed for help in finding the bear.

Moments later as I crawled through the tall grass and alders, I saw a patch of black. It looked like a small animal tucked into the grass. It was the bear. He had dug deep into the grassy marsh and nearly buried himself before he died. Only a small piece of his backside remained visible.

I went back to get Dave and tell him the good news, and he and I pulled and tugged that bear free and dragged him up the slope so I could cape him. It may not have been a trophy bear in the normal sense, but this was certainly a trophy bear to Dave and me, especially to Dave. In fact, Dave proudly displays that bear rug in his house to this very day.

I have seen Dave fearlessly face more adventure in the wilderness of Alaska than most two-armed men. I watched him accomplish what others can't do, amputee or not. This was a moment I will cherish for a lifetime.

It was a real pleasure for me to see how even simple hunting and fishing adventures helped Dave to regain his confidence as he began to build his new life. Adventures don't have to be intense to promote healing. Even the little challenges we face each day in life can be used to build character. God will meet us where we are and will take us as far as we are willing to go.

FOURTEEN

"We'll Make It, Boss!"

Pilots have a favorite saying: "There are old pilots and there are bold pilots, but there aren't any old, bold pilots!" Well, my pilot this year was a fifty-year-old Texan, thrice married. Hmm, I figured anyone that age and still trying and flying couldn't be too bad. Just for grins, let's call him Ted. Ted the Texan. Now, each year Ted flew his Piper PA-18 Cub from Texas to Alaska to be a bush pilot—or just maybe he was flying that far to get away from a fourth go-around with another one of those Texas gals! I'm not sure, but I got a little uneasy when I found out that Ted was hard of hearing. After meeting one of his ex-wives, I discovered he obviously couldn't see either. Hopefully he could fly.

I had just fished a large group from the "Lower 48." We'd had a great week, and, as is often the case, two of the guests, a father and son, wanted to expand their trip and hunt caribou and bear. Ted flew them up to Grizzly Ridge, along with one of my best guides. They landed without incident, set up camp, and eagerly got ready to hunt for a few days. They had top-quality tents and plenty of supplies and survival gear. I anticipated they would have an awesome time in a beautiful, remote spot.

Several days later, though, the weather turned ugly, and I decided to check on them. I knew it was a risk to fly in bad weather, but I needed to make sure my clients were OK. It was one thing to risk my own life in these conditions, but I would never ask a client to do the same.

On the way out to our plane, I stopped by my Alaskan Adventures "weather station." Many guides have something similar. Here is how it works: A beautiful piece of Alaskan hematite hangs from a hemp rope tied to a tree near the runway. I examine this stunning black rock carefully. If it is wet, well, it must be raining. If it is swaying, then it is surely windy—I have learned to gauge the wind's strength by how much it sways. If the hematite is hot, then it is sunny; if it is cool, then it is overcast. If it is bluish, it is very cold, and if white, then it is snowing. Now, if it is *gone* . . . then we had a tornado!

After my weather check—wildly swaying rock, indicating a strong wind—off Ted and I went. The wind made the landing tricky on the already tricky ridge, but Ted did an excellent job.

We had barely come to a stop when we got charged—not by a grizzly, but by the father! His clothes were flapping in the wind, his cap was cockeyed, snarled wisps of hair were blowing sideways, one boot was starting to come off, and he was spitting his words out like a hissing cat.

I scrambled out of the plane and strained to hear what he was saying. Was someone hurt? What was going on?

Finally, I could make out his words: "Take us back right now! Get us out of here! Where have you been? We want to go now! We don't want to stay here another night!"

I looked at him, startled. "Just *where* do you want me to fly you?"

Without missing a beat, and just as serious as you please, he said, "Take me to Detroit Metro!" Was this guy serious?

He was. I couldn't help myself. I cracked up. I could not stop laughing. My little plane could go maybe two hundred miles without filling up. We were over four *thousand* miles from Detroit. Had this guy been smoking something?

The more I laughed, the angrier he got. Realizing I needed to mollify him, I said, "Hey, I just came to check on you because the weather is bad. But I did bring extra supplies, and I even brought some candy bars." Meanwhile, I'm thinking, *Who is this guy? I'm risking my life to check on him. Where does he think he is?* Who *does he think he is?*

He just glared at me. Looking over his shoulder, I could see some caribou horns and the hide of a black bear nearby. I asked him if they had any success hunting. He yelled at me, "Yeah, we got two caribou and a bear. Now get us out of here!"

Wow! I thought. *A great week fishing, a successful hunt, a beautiful location, and he is fighting mad!* I started to get riled up because I could feel the confrontation in this guy. *OK, calm yourself. He isn't used to the real Alaska. Maybe he is scared.* I shook my head and said, "I'm very sorry, sir, but I can't fly you out right now. It's too windy. It would be too dangerous." Oh my, did the veins start bulging on his neck!

And then the strangest thing happened. He stomped right over to my plane and stood in front of its tail. Then I watched spellbound as he loaded up and spit—right on my Alaskan Adventures logo! *Right on my plane!* I couldn't believe it. He was a grown man, a business owner, a wealthy executive, and here he was, spitting on my plane! For once I was speechless. I wanted to grab his hat, wipe off the spit with it, and then slap it back on his balding head!

What is that other saying? Like father, like son? Well, you won't believe this. A moment later the son came storming out of the tent.

His face was red, and his shirt was buttoned all funny. His pants were half-zipped and starting to fall off. There is no way he could have seen what had transpired between his father and me, but somehow he had figured out they weren't leaving their camp. He was staring at me real hard and swinging his shoulders and arms aggressively as he headed toward my plane. I watched in disbelief as he marched straight to it.

No! This wasn't happening. He gathered himself up, reared his head back, and launched a huge spitball of his own, right on my plane! Who in blazes were these guys? And not only were they psycho, they had loaded guns!

Thinking Ted was right behind me, I turned my head slightly and said, "Ted, let's . . . uh . . . get outta here."

Ted was no dummy. He had stayed *in* the plane, keeping it revved up so that the wind would not blow us off the hill. I ran and jumped in too, wondering if that nasty spit from those two yahoos would eat a hole in the tail. Meanwhile, the yahoos were still yelling and, for added measure, giving us "the finger." I yelled out the window, more sweetly than called for, "We'll be back when it clears." I wanted to add, "*Maybe!*"

Ted had the plane facing the wind and got ready to take off. That couldn't happen soon enough to suit me!

It was then that I realized how much harder the wind seemed to be blowing. I prayed that we would be OK. I looked at Ted. His face was intent, he was gritting his teeth, and his lips were pressed tightly together. This was serious. We taxied, made a run at it, got pummeled by the wind, and then I felt liftoff. The plane was shaking, though, and we couldn't get any air speed. Instinctively, I knew we were too low.

We passed over the crest of the ridge and had just begun to achieve more lift when I heard a thump. We had hit the top of a tree obscured by the ridge. I think it was the only tree on that side of the hill. We hit it square, and the prop tore through some of the limbs and bark. Pine needles, branches, and debris bounced off the windshield. Miraculously the plane forged ahead and stayed airborne. I yelled, "What *was* that, Ted?"

"Uh . . . it's OK, boss," he answered. "That was just a little tree."

We continued to gain height, and I began to breathe easier as I saw the ground receding, but I wondered if that "little" fifteen-foot tree had damaged the plane or landing gear. Would we find out the hard way? My thoughts returned to the guys on the ground. They would probably love to see us crash!

In fact, part of the tree *had* slammed up inside the cowling and had broken the gasolator. We didn't know it yet, but we were leaking gas fast and would be out of fuel in no time. We climbed higher and higher, out over a canyon, and as we did I relaxed more, but I was still thinking about those two men. Why were they so angry? On the surface, it didn't make sense, but I realized in my heart that it was perfectly logical. I had seen it happen before. Powerful men who were in total control in the cutthroat world of business, who, with a word, simple gesture, or stroke of the pen, could make things happen—and quickly—suddenly found themselves alone, without resources, helpless, and no longer in control. Sometimes these men had never faced their internal fears and the aloneness they were forced to confront when thus isolated in the wild. The healing opportunity for these men and subsequent shift in priorities were often awesome, but I had learned healing would rarely occur unless initiated from within, never from without.

The thing that surprised me this time was that this had happened with a father and son *together*. Most fathers I know would give their right arm to experience such a dream hunting and fishing trip with their sons. Talk about quality time! Ted and I began talking about this when suddenly the plane engine sputtered, the whole frame shuddered, and the engine died.

The prop came to a standstill right before our eyes! We were almost a thousand feet in the air—and staring at a prop that was not moving. Talk about a sinking, hopeless feeling. Soon *we* would be sinking, and fast! I kept staring at the prop, our lifeline, trying to will it to start turning. Ted kept trying to crank the motor to get the plane restarted. The wind was blowing directly into us so hard that we actually began to glide.

Rrrnnnhhh, rrrnnnhhh. The plane was not going to start. We were completely out of gas. I yelled at Ted. "Turn downwind and go for the slope."

Thank God he refused to follow my advice. We would have picked up incredible speed, crashed into the hill headfirst, likely exploded in a ball of flames, and both died.

Ted kept the plane pointed directly into the wind, trying to get lift and knowing instinctively that it was the only way to keep our speed down and the nose up, while the plane wanted to crash straight down. Still we were descending rapidly and heading into the canyon.

As we gathered speed, I saw huge pine trees pointing straight up surrounding the canyon. "Oh no!" I yelled.

Ted began shouting right back, "We'll make it, boss. We'll make it!"

I screamed, "Ted, we aren't going to make it!"

But he kept repeating over and over, as if trying to convince himself, "We'll make it, boss! We'll make it!"

We were about fifteen seconds from impact, and they were some of the longest fifteen seconds of my life. I was sitting in the back, directly behind Ted. I grabbed my backpack and jammed it over my face. I knew the plane was made of a light material, and the black spruce trees would rip right through and into us. *Why couldn't we have landed where there were no trees?* I thought. *Why did I decide to check on those guys? How bad is this gonna hurt? "We're gonna make it, boss"? Ha! We* aren't *going to make it!*

Bam! The noise was horrendous as we crashed into the treetops. The plane spun and swung sideways, and the wings began breaking off. We plowed directly into a big spruce, and the engine smacked hard into the trunk. That stopped our forward progress. Then the landing gear came off; the wheels came up through the plane bottom, along with the struts, and slammed into me. The plane plummeted to the ground, nose first. *Bang!* Then everything was still.

I was dazed but quickly realized I was alive. I couldn't believe it! Alert now, I looked around, felt everything, pinched myself in a few places, and discovered I was still in one piece. I was in pain, but I knew I would be OK.

I forced the rear joystick aside and managed to crawl to Ted. His head was slumped on his chest, his face was lacerated and bloody, and his eyes were closed. Ted was out cold. At first I thought he was dead. Gas was all over the plane, and the smell hit me. It struck me how eerie and deathly quiet it was after all the noise.

Ted's nose was bent and bleeding. I got him loose from his seat belt and could feel that his right leg was rubbery and broken. I saw that his left foot was twisted too.

Suddenly I became aware that he was breathing! I could hear and feel the faint air from his lips as I moved him out of the plane. My heart leaped in my chest. Ted was alive too!

I dragged him from the plane, and as I did, he began to moan and come to. I pulled him to the back and leaned him up against the tail, then sat on the plane for a while and gathered strength.

Ted shifted his weight, and I leaned in close to him and said, "Ted, I think we're done; we're finished." And then, for reasons I don't fully comprehend, I said, "Ted, God was talking to one of us, and He was trying to get our attention. God was trying to tell us something." I added, "I want to tell you something, Ted. Right now, I thought I was going to die. I thought I would be in heaven and I was going to see Jesus." I continued quietly, "Ted, did you think that?"

Through his bloody mouth he gasped out groggily, "No. I don't know . . ." He paused for a few moments, took some breaths, and, almost as if in a daze, said, "Rock, you know, when I was young, I went to a small Baptist church in Texas. They told me all about salvation. My mom used to pray that I would get saved."

I did not know the extent of Ted's injuries and suddenly felt an inner presence prompting me to share the gospel with him. I said, "Ted, *are* you saved?"

He replied firmly, "No, I'm not."

I said, "Ted, do you want to bow your head right now and pray the sinner's prayer with me?"

He nodded slowly and bowed his head. I then led him through a simple prayer of repentance, and he accepted the Lord. Our plane was down and torn up, and Ted's body was broken and brutalized, but he immediately seemed to have a new spirit. Even with his injuries and through his pain, he exhibited a new look and visibly gained strength and confidence. I have rarely felt such a strong spiritual presence.

Our emergency locator transmitter (ELT) had gone off when we crashed, and several brave pilots rushed out to try and find us. One seasoned pilot who saw the wreckage told everyone over his radio, "They gotta be dead. They just gotta be." He could not see how anyone could have survived that crash. That's how bad it looked from the air. And his were the first words that my wife, family, and friends heard about our crash. Were they ever stunned and joyful when they learned we were alive!

I hurried to gather some emergency gear from the plane. As Ted got stronger, I pulled him up and put his arms around my shoulder and was able to laboriously drag/carry him to a place where we knew a plane could land. Jeremy Davis, one of the best bush pilots in Alaska, negotiated the bad weather, flew in, landed, and amazingly airlifted us out in one trip, though his plane normally carries only one passenger at a time. On the ride back I asked him, "Jeremy, is God mad at me? Is He punishing me?"

"In this line of work, these things are going to happen," Jeremy answered. "God knows that this is inherent in the life we have chosen. In *life* things happen. We can never ask why with an angry, raised fist, but rather with a broken heart and a sense of faith." These words meant a lot to me then and often have during other intense times in my life. And I continue to realize how precious life is when I face the reality of losing it.

We finally got the father and son off Grizzly Ridge. Whether they were angry with each other or something else, they never said, but they certainly had wanted to leave immediately. Maybe they had become afraid of the wilderness once in it. On the rare occasions when this happens, I try to accommodate, but safety is always first. So how did they thank me for refusing to let them fly out and probably saving their lives? They demanded all of their money back. What did I do? I refunded every nickel. They had spit on my plane. I didn't want them spitting on my life too.

I gotta be honest with you: I just don't get it. An Alaskan adventure by definition is not a slice of the civilized world and carries no guarantees of typical work schedules or timetables. The absence of the comforts of home often pushes a man to his core, to experience real manhood. Our culture as a whole, in my opinion, doesn't prepare young men to even *want* to seek their essence as a man, or to test themselves with real adventure. I would say that, especially in this case, it was an opportunity lost.

T. Davis Bunn in *Shadow of Victory* said that, "He was a safe man. One who never took any risk. Someone who always wears a hat when it is raining. He does everything by his book and lives a dull boring life of tranquility." Bunn may as well have written that about today's man.

Deep inside every person, in spite of upbringing, is a yearning to live on the edge, to experience the thrill of real adventure, and to find out who they are in the process. I think, in this culture of ambitions, we forget to pursue who we were made to be, something deeper than a nameplate on a desk or a college degree from a prestigious school. I believe that every person that allows their mettle to be tested in the wilderness learns secrets within that may not be revealed any other way.

FIFTEEN

Musings from a Guide

I am sitting in a warm, comfortable lodge in remote Alaska. My fire is crackling, and I have a cup of percolated coffee in my hand (not dripped; there *is* a difference). In a few hours, an excited hunter and I will jump into my plane, and my pilot will land us on a remote, wild mountain in Alaska. Our grizzly bear hunt will begin there. Will it be an adventure? You bet. And both my client's spirit and mine will be recharged after this hunt. Why is this?

Meaningful adventures bring deep reflection to our lives. On an adventure in a place like Alaska, you suddenly find yourself asking many questions: Why am I here? Why did I survive? What is driving me? Why do I collect wealth? Am I the person I should be? Am I right with my family, my friends, my coworkers? Am I right with God?

Adventures naturally cause introspection, and close encounters with death may motivate us to embrace change. Exciting, unusual experiences often evoke bold and risky yet positive lifestyle modifications. But an adventure certainly doesn't have to be life-threatening to be life-changing. Your nearest interstate is probably more dangerous than the Alaskan wilderness. Statistics certainly reflect this.

Yet I believe the wilderness is God's premier stage for changing hearts. Observing His creation can inspire you to worship and to trust His plan for your life.

My experiences have shown me that when people truly seek to "find themselves," too often what they find is a selfishness and self-willed life that they abhor. It is in precisely in that moment of revelation that life-changing and life-giving choices can be made. I know, because it is a journey that I, too, am taking.

This isn't a big riddle, and the adventures I've shared with you are truly much more than hunting and fishing stories. They are about discovering something real and finding your heart. Being in touch with nature can produce that.

In fact, consider why there is such a market for travel and recreation. We visit and explore exotic places. We stand in awe of the Grand Canyon and marvel at Mount Denali in the Alaska Range. We soak up sunshine on the beautiful beaches of the world, hike to mountain streams, or gaze at the midnight sky, lit up with thousands of stars. We are mesmerized by these awesome works of art. We may not even be aware why, but I believe it is because the soul of every person cries out for intimacy with the One who created these marvelous works. We are attracted to the wonders He has created because they demonstrate His complex love and care for all of His creation. Surely, if the Creator takes care of even the smallest of His creatures, He will take care of you and me.

But it is not enough to gaze in wonder at God's creation. True life and healing require going the next step: getting to know God personally and letting Him create a masterpiece with *your* life. It involves recognizing your need for Him, and for His Son, Jesus Christ, whom He sacrificed for us. And yes, it involves letting go and allowing Christ to make us the real men and women we are created to be.

The greatest adventure of my life did not begin when I became a guide, got married, or became the father of four precious daughters. My greatest adventure began when I trusted my heart and my life to Jesus and His plans for me. Maybe this sounds unusual to you, but my life with Jesus has been thrilling. It has been uncertain many times, but it has never been dull. Alaska has been the landscape of my spiritual upbringing. It was my home as a child and my rite of passage as a man and a breadwinner for my family. Though this life may seem more wild than most, it's just my particular place to encounter God and be impacted by the gospel of Jesus.

You have your place too.

If you want to find your life's significance and the purpose for which you were made, begin this adventure for yourself, an adventure with the Creator of the universe. After all, He made you, and He knows the unique person you are—and were meant to be. I promise that you will discover and enjoy the greatest adventures of your life by walking arm in arm with our Savior and Creator, Jesus Christ.

Take the adventurous risk to encounter Jesus and you'll begin your own trek that's as wild as Alaska, maybe wilder.

Tight Lines, Straight Shots,
Rocky

Acknowledgments

The Lord is good, a stronghold in the day of trouble and He knows those who take refuge in Him.

— NAHHUM 1:7

It was a Divine appointment. . . . Matt Jacobson, an observant agent, led me to Thomas Nelson. Thank you to my brother, Greg Bilbo. I believe God gifted your role in remembering, laughing, recalling and writing with me about our Alaskan journey. My deepest heartfelt thanks and respect.

Fishing and Hunting in Alaska

· What to Bring – What to Wear ·

Fishing: Guided

Comfortable warm pants: 2-3 pair

3 warm long sleeve shirts; 1-2 short
sleeve shirts

Tennis shoes and walking boots/shoes

Wool socks/heavy duty

Light thermal underwear

Warm jacket/sweaters

Personal toilet articles

Mosquito repellent (Cutters is good)
(May want net)

Hat/glasses/light gloves

Camera/film w/ case

All weather rain gear (See Bass Pro
Stores)

Fishing Pliers *(A MUST)

Polarized Fishing Glasses

King Salmon

Casting Rod/Reel: Lamiglas G1318T
or G1316T and Shimano TRN 200 G

Spinning Rod/Reel: Lamiglas G1319
and Penn 650 or 850SS

Dai Riki Monofilament 30 or 36 lb.
test or Maxima Monofilament 20 or
25 lb.

Extra line

Leader Wheels 46 lb. Dai Riki or 30
lb. Maxima

Rosco Snap Swivels Size 5 or 7

Pencil lead 1/4"

Pixee 7/8 oz. Hammered
Brass/Orange, Hammered
Nickel/Red

Spin-N-Glo Kits Size 2 or Size 0
Pink, Flame, Pearl/Red

Hot Shot 025 Orange, Silver, Blue Pirate

Magnum Tadpolly Nickel/Blue, Red, Nickel

Magnum Wiggle Wart

Krocodile 1 3/4 oz chartreuse or chrome

Tee Spoon #5 and Skagit Special #6

Vibrax Spinner Size 6 Silver, Silver/Red

Mepps Giant Killer

Single Siwash Hooks 3/0 4/0

Hook File

Lure Box

Scissors or Clippers

Polarized Fishing Glasses

Long Nose Pliers

Swiss Army Knife

Fishing Vest or Hip Pack

Chums, Silvers, Sockeyes, Large Char, and Steelhead

Casting Rod/Reel: Lamiglas G 1306T and Quantum 1420

Spinning Rod/Reel: Lamiglas G1307 and Penn 450SS

Dai Riki Monofilament 19 lb. test or Maxima Monofilament 12 lb. test

Extra line

Dai Riki Leader Wheels 15 and 19 test

Rosco Snap Swivels Size 10 and 7

Pixee 1/2 oz and 7/8 oz Silver/Red Silver/Green

Steelee 1/2 oz Metallic Green, HB/FL Stripe, HN/FL

Little Cleo 3/4 oz

Maribou Jigs 1/4 oz Red/White, Pink

Mepps Silver & Gold Size 5

Roostertail 1/2 oz Flame

Tee Spoon Size 4

Vibrax size 5 Silver or Silver/Green

Twist On Lead Strips and Split Shot

Hook File

Lure Box

Scissors or Clippers

Polarized Fishing Glasses

Long Nose Pliers

Swiss Army Knife

Fishing Vest or Hip Pack

Single Siwash Hooks 1/0, 2/0, 3/0

Rainbows, Char and Grayling

Spinning Rod/Reel: Lamiglas G1212 and Penn 430SS

Dai-Riki Monofilament 12 test or Maxima 8 lb. test

Extra line

Leader Wheels 10 lb. test Dai Riki

Rosco Lock Snap Swivel Size 10

Pixee 1/2 oz Hammered Brass/Orange, and Hammered Nickel/Red

Steelee 1/2 oz HamBr/Fl Stripe, or HamNi/Fl Stripe

Maribou Jigs 1/4 oz Red /White, Black

Roostertail 1/8 oz and 1/4 oz Flame, White, or Yellow

Shyster Spinners Fire/Black Dot 1/3 oz

Mepps Spinners Silver or Gold Size 3

Vibrax Spinners Silver Size 3

Single Siwash Hooks Size 2 and 1/0

Single Egg Fly-Peachy King, Alaskan Roe, Baby Pink, & Salmon Egg Size 6

Twist On Lead Strips and split shot

Hook File

Lure Box Scissors or Clippers

Polarized Fishing Glasses

Long Nose Pliers

Swiss Army Knife Fishing Vest or Hip Pack

Fly-Fishing

King Salmon (Fly-Fishing)

Rod: Lamiglas G1298-9 or G1299-9

Reels: SA System II 1011 or 89

Extra Spool

Fly line backing 30 lb.

Teeny 300 and Wet Tip Lines

Tapered Leaders 16 and 20 lb. tippets

Dai Riki Leader Wheels .017 and .019

Twist On Lead & Split Shot

Hook File

Fly Box

Scissors or Clippers

Polarized Sun Glasses

Long Nose Pliers

Swiss Army Knife Fishing Vest

Outrageous 4/0

Crazy Charlie Purple Pearl 4/0

Polar Shrimp 1/0

Teeny Nymph Size 2 Pink, Flame, Black, Ginger

Alaskabous, Pixees Revenge, Showgirl Size 1/0

Wiggle Tail Orange or Pink Size 1/0

Chums, Silvers, Sockeyes, Large Char, and Steelhead (Fly-Fishing)

Rods: Lamiglas G1298-8

Reels: S.A. System II 78, PFlueger Medalist 1495 1/2 Hardy St. Aidan and Marguis 10

Extra spools

Fly Line Backing

Floating, Wet tip and T300 Teeny lines

Tapered Leaders 12 lb. Tippet

Dai Riki Leader Wheels .013 to .015

Twist on Lead Strips & Split Shot

Hook File

Fly Box

Scissors or Clippers

Polarized Fishing Glasses

Long Nose Pliers

Swiss Army Knife

Fishing Vest

Alaskan Bug Eyes Size 2

G String Size 2

Teeny Nymph Size 2 Pink, Flame, Black, Ginger

Babine Special Size 2 & 4

Skykomish Sunrise Size 2

Bright Roe Pink Size 2

Polar Shrimp Size 2 & 4

Outrageous 1/0

Alaskabous, Show Girl, Pixee Revenge, Coho Size 1/0

Woolly Bugger Purple Size 2

Rainbows, Char, and Grayling (Fly-Fishing)

Rods: Lamiglas G1297-6 or G1298-6

Reels: SA System II 67 PFlueger 1495 Hardy Princess Backing

Floating, Wet tip, and T200 Teeny Lines

Tapered leaders 6 and 8 lb. tippet

Dai Riki leader wheels .008, .009, .010, .011

Twist On lead strips & Split Shot

Strike indicators

Fly floatant

Line cleaner

Hook file

Fly box

Scissors or clippers

Polarized fishing glasses

Long nose pliers

Swiss Army Knife

Fishing Vest

Single Egg Flies Size 6 Peachy King, Alaskan Roe, Baby Pink, and Salmon Egg

Woolly Worms Size 2 & 4 Black/Black, and Grizzly/Black

Black Maribou Muddler Size 4

Black Matuka Size 2

Matuka Sculpin Size 2, Olive

Teeny Nymph Size 4 Pink, Flame, Black, Ginger

Black Maribou Leach Size 2

Mouserat

Wiggle Lemming

Babine Special Size 4, 6, and 8

Polar Shrimp Size 4

Bitch Creek Size 4 and 6

Girdle Bug Size 4

Woolly Bugger Size 2 and 4 Black

Muddler Minnow Size 4 and 6

Black Gnat Size 16 Grayling

Mosquito Size 16

Humpy Size 12

Wulff Grizzly and Royal Size 10

Bright Roe Orange Size 4

Egg Sucking Leech Size 4 Purple and Black

Hunting: Guided

Thick layers of warm waterproof clothing, not bulky heavy coats, etc. The river and mountain hunting is cold. Your feet and hands are most important, so bring wool: no substitutes.

All gear, including rifle, should not weigh more than 50 lbs. per person. All flying is done in small aircraft and space and weight is at a premium. All clothing should be packed in soft sided duffel canvas bags. Rifles should be in soft cases.

Note: Soft cases for rifles are allowed on bush planes but not on most commercial flights.

Warm heavy duty waterproof Gortex rain gear. (Columbia or Browning brands are suggested)

(Raingear must be quiet and camouflage for successful trophy hunting.)

2-3 comfortable warm pants

3-4 warm long sleeve shirts

Tennis shoes, walking boots, or hunting boots

Wool socks/heavy duty

Thermal underwear

Warm Jacket/Sweaters

Personal toilet articles

Mosquito repellent (Cutters is good)

Hat/glasses/warm Gortex gloves

Camera/Film

Ammo, Rifle

Fishing license-if you plan to fish

  (*May order online at*
  www.adfg.state.ak.us)

Binoculars

Game bags (a must)

Skinning knives

License and tags for moose, caribou, grizzly/brown bear, or black bear.

Must have prior to arrival at hunting area! They cannot be shared between hunters.

(*May order online at*
www.adfg.state.ak.us*)*

About the Author

Rocky McElveen and his wife, Sharon, are owners of Alaskan Adventures (www.alaskan-adventures.com). Rocky, a seminary graduate and the son of an Alaskan missionary, was raised in Alaska and knows its charm and challenges better than anyone. For twenty years he has been a professional guide in that wild state. His knowledge of the primitive frontier, along with his warm, hospitable manner, adds an unprecedented dimension to his credentials as a master fishing, and registered hunting guide. He is esteemed as friend by many who have been under his guide: President George Bush Sr.; General Charles E. "Chuck" Yeager; major league baseball player Dave Dravecky; Bob Seiple, president of World Vision; Pastor Chuck Swindoll; and Oakland A's pitcher Mike Moore, to only name a few.

Rocky travels and speaks at retreats, churches, high schools, and wild game dinners. To inquire about Rocky's availability or to learn more about wild game dinners, go to www.wildmenwildalaska.com